Psychotic Temptation

How can we understand the pull towards that which we fear: psychosis?

In this thought-provoking book, Abensour proposes the idea of a temptation towards psychosis rather than a regression, as a response to the hatred or denial of the subject's origins. She shares her reflections on her psychoanalytic work with psychotic patients focusing on their struggle to achieve a coherent sense of a self that can inhabit a shared world. Abensour locates this struggle within the universal human struggle to achieve a balance between what we can and cannot allow ourselves to know about the reality of death and of our insignificance in the world.

Liliane Abensour was a lecturer at the Faculty of English at the University of Paris VII, a training member of the Paris Psychoanalytic Society and co-editor of the journal of the Centre Kestemberg, *Psychoanalysis and Psychosis*.

THE NEW LIBRARY OF PSYCHOANALYSIS
General Editor: Alessandra Lemma

The New Library of Psychoanalysis was launched in 1987 in association with the Institute of Psychoanalysis, London. It took over from the International Psychoanalytical Library which published many of the early translations of the works of Freud and the writings of most of the leading British and Continental psychoanalysts.

The purpose of the New Library of Psychoanalysis is to facilitate a greater and more widespread appreciation of psychoanalysis and to provide a forum for increasing mutual understanding between psychoanalysts and those working in other disciplines such as the social sciences, medicine, philosophy, history, linguistics, literature and the arts. It aims to represent different trends both in British psychoanalysis and in psychoanalysis generally. The New Library of Psychoanalysis is well placed to make available to the English-speaking world psychoanalytic writings from other European countries and to increase the interchange of ideas between British and American psychoanalysts. Through the *Teaching Series*, the New Library of Psychoanalysis now also publishes books that provide comprehensive, yet accessible, overviews of selected subject areas aimed at those studying psychoanalysis and related fields such as the social sciences, philosophy, literature and the arts.

The Institute, together with the British Psychoanalytical Society, runs a low-fee psychoanalytic clinic, organizes lectures and scientific events concerned with psychoanalysis and publishes the *International Journal of Psychoanalysis.* It runs the a training course in psychoanalysis which leads to membership of the International Psychoanalytical Association – the body which preserves internationally agreed standards of training, of professional entry, and of professional ethics and practice for psychoanalysis as initiated and developed by Sigmund Freud. Distinguished members of the Institute have included Michael Balint, Wilfred Bion, Ronald Fairbairn, Anna Freud, Ernest Jones, Melanie Klein, John Rickman and Donald Winnicott.

Previous general editors have included David Tuckett, who played a very active role in the establishment of the New Library. He was followed as general editor by Elizabeth Bott Spillius, who was in turn followed by Susan Budd and then by Dana Birksted-Breen.

ALSO IN THIS SERIES

Impasse and Interpretation Herbert Rosenfeld
Psychoanalysis and Discourse Patrick Mahony
The Suppressed Madness of Sane Men Marion Milner
The Riddle of Freud Estelle Roith
Thinking, Feeling, and Being Ignacio Matte Blanco
The Theatre of the Dream Salomon Resnik
Melanie Klein Today: Volume 1, Mainly Theory Edited by Elizabeth Bott Spillius
Melanie Klein Today: Volume 2, Mainly Practice Edited by Elizabeth Bott Spillius
Psychic Equilibrium and Psychic Change: Selected Papers of Betty Joseph Edited by Michael Feldman and Elizabeth Bott Spillius
About Children and Children-No-Longer: Collected Papers 1942–80 Paula Heimann. Edited by Margret Tonnesmann
The Freud–Klein Controversies 1941–45 Edited by Pearl King and Riccardo Steiner
Dream, Phantasy and Art Hanna Segal
Psychic Experience and Problems of Technique Harold Stewart
Clinical Lectures on Klein & Bion Edited by Robin Anderson
From Fetus to Child Alessandra Piontelli
A Psychoanalytic Theory of Infantile Experience: Conceptual and Clinical Reflections E Gaddini. Edited by Adam Limentani
The Dream Discourse Today Edited and introduced by Sara Flanders
The Gender Conundrum: Contemporary Psychoanalytic Perspectives on Feminitity and Masculinity Edited and introduced by Dana Breen
Psychic Retreats John Steiner
The Taming of Solitude: Separation Anxiety in Psychoanalysis Jean-Michel Quinodoz
Unconscious Logic: An Introduction to Matte-Blanco's Bi-logic and its Uses Eric Rayner
Understanding Mental Objects Meir Perlow
Life, Sex and Death: Selected Writings of William Gillespie Edited and introduced by Michael Sinason
What Do Psychoanalysts Want?: The Problem of Aims in Psychoanalytic Therapy Joseph Sandler and Anna Ursula Dreher
Michael Balint: Object Relations, Pure and Applied Harold Stewart
Hope: A Shield in the Economy of Borderline States Anna Potamianou
Psychoanalysis, Literature & War: Papers 1972–1995 Hanna Segal
Emotional Vertigo: Between Anxiety and Pleasure Danielle Quinodoz
Early Freud and Late Freud Ilse Grubrich-Simitis
A History of Child Psychoanalysis Claudine and Pierre Geissmann
Belief and Imagination: Explorations in Psychoanalysis Ronald Britton

A Mind of One's Own: A Psychoanalytic View of Self and Object Robert A Caper
Psychoanalytic Understanding of Violence and Suicide Edited by Rosine Jozef Perelberg
On Bearing Unbearable States of Mind Ruth Riesenberg-Malcolm
Psychoanalysis on the Move: The Work of Joseph Sandler Edited by Peter Fonagy, Arnold M. Cooper and Robert S. Wallerstein
The Dead Mother: The Work of André Green Edited by Gregorio Kohon
The Fabric of Affect in the Psychoanalytic Discourse André Green
The Bi-Personal Field: Experiences of Child Analysis Antonino Ferro
The Dove that Returns, the Dove that Vanishes: Paradox and Creativity in Psychoanalysis Michael Parsons
Ordinary People, Extra-ordinary Protections: A Post Kleinian Approach to the Treatment of Primitive Mental States Judith Mitrani
The Violence of Interpretation: From Pictogram to Statement Piera Aulagnier
The Importance of Fathers: A Psychoanalytic Re-Evaluation Judith Trowell and Alicia Etchegoyen
Dreams That Turn Over a Page: Paradoxical Dreams in Psychoanalysis Jean-Michel Quinodoz
The Couch and the Silver Screen: Psychoanalytic Reflections on European Cinema Andrea Sabbadini
In Pursuit of Psychic Change: The Betty Joseph Workshop Edited by Edith Hargreaves and Arturo Varchevker
The Quiet Revolution in American Psychoanalysis: Selected Papers of Arnold M. Cooper Arnold M. Cooper, Edited and Introduced by Elizabeth L. Auchincloss
Seeds of Illness and Seeds of Recovery: The genesis of suffering and the role of psychoanalysis Antonino Ferro
The Work of Psychic Figurability: Mental States Without Representation César Botella and Sára Botella
Key Ideas for a Contemporary Psychoanalysis: Misrecognition and Recognition of the Unconscious André Green
The Telescoping of Generations: Listening to the Narcissistic Links Between Generations Haydée Faimberg
Glacial Times: A Journey through the World of Madness Salomon Resnik
This Art of Psychoanalysis: Dreaming Undreamt Dreams and Interrupted Cries Thomas H Ogden
Psychoanalysis and Religion in the 21st Century: Competitors or Collaborators? David M. Black
Recovery of the Lost Good Object Eric Brenman
The Many Voices of Psychoanalysis Roger Kennedy
Feeling the Words: Neuropsychoanalytic Understanding of Memory and the Unconscious Mauro Mancia
Constructions and the Analytic Field: History, Scenes and Destiny Domenico Chianese

Projected Shadows: Psychoanalytic Reflections on the Representation of Loss in European Cinema Edited by Andrea Sabbadini
Encounters with Melanie Klein: Selected Papers of Elizabeth Spillius Elizabeth Spillius
Yesterday, Today and Tomorrow Hanna Segal
Psychoanalysis Comparable and Incomparable: The Evolution of a Method to Describe and Compare Psychoanalytic Approaches David Tuckett, Roberto Basile, Dana Birksted-Breen, Tomas Böhm, Paul Denis, Antonino Ferro, Helmut Hinz, Arne Jemstedt, Paola Mariotti and Johan Schubert
Time, Space and Phantasy Rosine Jozef Perelberg
Rediscovering Psychoanalysis: Thinking and Dreaming, Learning and Forgetting Thomas H. Ogden
Mind Works: Techniques and Creativity in Psychoanalysis Antonino Ferro
Doubt Conviction and the Analytic Process: Selected Papers of Michael Feldman Michael Feldman
Melanie Klein in Berlin: Her First Psychoanalyses of Children Claudia Frank
The Psychotic Wavelength: A Psychoanalytic Perspective for Psychiatry Richard Lucas
Betweenity: A Discussion of the Concept of Borderline Judy Gammelgaard
The Intimate Room: Theory and Technique of the Analytic Field Giuseppe Civitarese
Bion Today Edited by Chris Mawson
Secret Passages: The Theory and Technique of Interpsychic Relations Stefano Bolognini
Intersubjective Processes and the Unconscious: An Integration of Freudian, Kleinian and Bionian Perspectives Lawrence J. Brown
Seeing and Being Seen: Emerging from a Psychic Retreat John Steiner
Avoiding Emotions, Living Emotions Antonio Ferro
Projective Identification: The Fate of a Concept Edited by Elizabeth Spillius and Edna O'Shaughnessy
Creative Readings: Essays on Seminal Analytic Works Thomas Ogden
The Maternal Lineage Edited by Paola Mariotti
Donald Winnicott Today Edited by Jan Abram
Symbiosis and Ambiguity: A Psychoanalytic Study Edited by John Churcher, José Bleger and Leopoldo Bleger
Psychotic Temptation Liliane Abensour
The Theory and Technique of Psychoanalytic Supervision: The Sao Paulo Clinical Seminars Antonino Ferro

TITLES IN THE NEW LIBRARY OF PSYCHOANALYSIS TEACHING SERIES

Reading Freud: A Chronological Exploration of Freud's Writings Jean-Michel Quinodoz

Listening to Hanna Segal: Her Contribution to Psychoanalysis Jean-Michel Quinodoz
Reading French Psychoanalysis Edited by Dana Birksted-Breen, Sara Flanders and Alain Gibeault
Reading Winnicott Lesley Caldwell and Angela Joyce
Initiating Psychoanalysis: Perspectives Bernard Reith, Sven Lagerlöf, Penelope Crick, Mette Møller and Elisabeth Skale
Infant Observation Frances Salo
Reading Anna Freud Nick Midgley

TITLES IN THE NEW LIBRARY OF PSYCHOANALYSIS 'BEYOND THE COUCH' SERIES

Under the Skin: A Psychoanalytic Study of Body Modification Alessandra Lemma
Engaging with Climate Change: Psychoanalytic and Interdisciplinary Perspectives Edited by Sally Weintrobe

Psychotic Temptation

Liliane Abensour

Translated by David Alcorn

Routledge
Taylor & Francis Group
LONDON AND NEW YORK

First published 2013
by Routledge
4 Park Square, Milton Park, Abingdon, Oxon OX14 4RN
605 Third Avenue, New York, NY 10017

Routledge is an imprint of the Taylor & Francis Group, an informa business

British Library Cataloguing in Publication Data
A catalogue record for this book is available from the British Library

Library of Congress Cataloging in Publication Data

Abensour, Liliane.
[Tentation psychotique. English]
Psychotic temptation / Liliane Abensour ; translated by David Alcorn.
p. cm. – (The new library of psychoanalysis)

Includes bibliographical references and index.
1. Psychoses. 2. Psychoanalysis. 3. Mental illness. I. Title.
RC512.A2413 2012

616.89'17—dc23 2012021781

ISBN: 978-0-415-67321-1 (hbk)
ISBN: 978-0-415-67322-8 (pbk)
ISBN: 978-0-203-07882-2 (ebk)

Typeset in Bembo
by RefineCatch Ltd, Bungay, Suffolk

Contents

Foreword by Bernard Chervet

This foreword is a tribute to Liliane Abensour. It is the second time that I have presented this compilation of her thoughts on psychosis. When I first did so, she was still alive and indeed present on that occasion. This foreword is thus marked by feelings of pain.

Her book brings together the three dimensions of thinking – emotional, figurative and theoretical. With these, she has combined her highly respectful attentiveness towards the tragic experience of her psychotic patients, her familiarity with psychoanalytic writing on the subject and her knowledge of literature and art.[1]

That approach is in line with the two great traditions that have marked psychiatry: *humanism*,[2] with its acknowledgement of the existence of a human being inside every insane person, and *phenomenology*, in particular transcendental phenomenology, Binswanger's *Daseinanalyse.*

This book should be looked upon as a work of research. It is skilfully written, precise and well balanced. The author does not attempt to hide just how enigmatic, for psychiatrists and psychoanalysts, the psychotic solution is, or with what degree of delicacy it must be approached.

The underlying psychotic potentiality

What Liliane Abensour studies in this book is not psychosis as such but what she calls the *psychotic temptation*, i.e. the potentiality that every human being possesses and which can be called upon as a psychical response to deal with the traumatic dimension that lies within every one of us from birth onwards.

She writes (*infra*, p. 135): "To talk in terms of a delusional temptation . . . enables us to take into consideration the various forms that delusional thinking – or thinking that is almost but not quite delusional – can take. It also implies that the boundary that separates delusional thinking from other kinds – and from poetic thinking in particular – is an uncertain one, one that is inherently mobile. Behind all of these kinds of thinking lies the fundamental and always enigmatic question that human beings evoke – the origins and meaning of life, of oneself, of the world – as well as the many attempts to answer it, either in part or as a whole."

Liliane Abensour adopts a twofold approach. She sees that traumatic constraint as being part of every individual in his or her development, defined as a crossroads of various temptations, and the psychotic temptation as following on from the collapse and subsequent loss of spatial and temporal markers.

It was her experience with adult psychotics that encouraged her to follow those two pathways. Child psychiatrists have a different kind of experience – that of very early attempts at psychotic solutions, long before the concepts of space and time have been integrated. Adult psychosis is a form of pathology that belongs to a subsequent phase, much later, long after a considerable number of developmental steps have been covered.

Liliane Abensour rejects any idea of attributing the determinism of psychosis simply to an individual's personal history. She does not see psychosis as being the return of substitutes, as is the case with neurotic symptoms. The question that remains open is therefore that of the part played by memory, especially since, in her view, the psychotic temptation involves the primary workings of the mind.

She rejects also the idea of impermeability put forward in structural conceptions, preferring to make room for some randomness between the various solutions to which an individual may have recourse. If these bear the hallmark of some degree of subservience to the individual's past history and lifestyle, she argues that they should be seen as potentialities that possess some degree of mutual flexibility.

The psychotic temptation is, therefore, part of ordinary clinical phenomena. This is in line with what Freud wrote in 1939: "A dream . . . is a psychosis" – normal, harmless and even indispensable.

Liliane Abensour argues that if, in our theoretical approach to psychosis and its treatment, we continue to refer to the neuroses and to borderline states, this will only lead to a technical and theoretical dead-end. Drawing on the work of psychoanalysts such as Winnicott and Bion, she says that some childhood experiences have not been properly registered or inscribed in the sphere of the mind and are therefore *missing, lacking.* These experiences have remained outside of any desire or memory, but they may be approached through a psychoanalytic and emotional relationship.

Freud had the idea that these missing experiences could be deduced from hallucinatory impressions and effects that are expressed in the course of an analytical session, making use of material bordering on those that are missing. It is therefore more a question of psychical processes having to do with a denial of existence. The development of such an individual involves contact with denial, as distinct from contact with a denied part of reality. Hence the absence of differentiation and the threat of breakdown when such denials begin to weaken (feelings of emptiness, states of confusion, depersonalization, etc.).

Liliane Abensour agrees that one part of the psychotic solution, the construction of a delusion, makes use of the infantile dimension discovered via the neuroses and narcissistic pathologies. Material from the infantile sphere is made use of as a response to the primary deficiency which is that of psychosis, hence the recurrence of sexual themes and ideas of grandeur. It is this recourse to the infantile aspects of sexuality and narcissism that lies at the heart of some of Freud's mistaken views on psychosis. In his study of Schreber (1911) and that of a case of paranoia running counter to the psychoanalytic theory of the disease (1915d), he describes delusions in terms of the logics of a symptom linked to repressed homosexuality, although he says also that there is some distortion of the ego with a specific kind of projection, in the sense of something suppressed internally coming back externally. Psychosis, therefore, for Freud, was a pathological form of narcissism. In 1924 he went on to differentiate the three main nosographic categories: neuroses, narcissistic pathologies and psychoses.

These developments in his thinking went hand-in-hand with the ever more detailed exploration of dream-theory. He therefore established a close connection between neurosis and hallucinatory wish-fulfilment, between narcissistic psychoneurosis and the function of the guardian of sleep, and between psychosis and the construction of neo-perceptions. The concept of splitting of the ego anticipated what we now consider to be psychical functioning in *fragmented topographies* (Chervet, 2008).

Liliane Abensour makes use not only of all of these ideas that Freud contributed, but also of what a great many of his successors[3] have handed down, especially Evelyne Kestemberg. Her focus is on the primal, original moment, when the psychotic temptation appears as a virtuality.

It is only towards the end of her book that she discusses the attempt at self-cure specific to psychosis that we refer to as the construction of a delusion. The major part of her work focuses on the immobilization and exacerbation that the individual may be forced to accept from the very beginning of his or her life. It is in circumstances such as those that the psychotic temptation may come to the fore.

Theoretical issues

It follows from this that a certain number of questions run all through this book. About the status of thing-presentations, the differentiation between memory traces based on perceptions, their respective roles in the economic modalities that are constituent parts of memory; about the traumatic dimension that lies – to use a well-known phrase – beyond the pleasure principle; about the concept of reality, and the conflict between a passive perception that imposes itself upon the individual and the perceptual category that is built up from a hallucinatory aspect; about that other pole, the processual one, the function of which is to respond to the traumatic attraction that lies within and between the drives; about the dissociation between two poles – the traumatic aspect of the drives and the processual response that is the foundation of the psychical sphere; about the capacity to saturate via a neo-perception the internal surface of consciousness in order to lend support to the denial of that which, in perception, has a traumatic impact; about the interaction between external reality-perception and the internal reality-perceptual dimension; about the implications of generating and creating within the psychical apparatus, etc.

These questions lead to a re-thinking of one of the functions of dreams from which the psychotic solution takes support – the fact of having to impose a perceptual neo-reality on the sleeper's consciousness. That is what dreams have to do – to treat the traumatic dimension that is part of the duality of the drives. The psychotic temptation takes support from the mind's ability to create a perceptual world, one in which nothing is lacking, one that runs parallel to a perception that cannot escape the reality of what is missing.

Libidinal cathexes, topographical structuring, liminal inscribing

We come upon those questions in the very headings of the three Parts and eight chapters of this book. Through them, Liliane Abensour explores the fundamental axes that are constitutive of the psychotic temptation: the temporal axis, the spatial one and the vertigo of creation.

Part III is the most original of the three. It focuses on how the creativeness of the mind operates, and draws a parallel between art and delusion.

Part I, the temporal axis, focuses on cathexes: how they come about, what becomes of them, the conflicts that are part of them from the very beginning, as well as their fluctuations, dynamic aspects and discontinuities. Often, the author prefers to discuss these aspects via the notion of time and the psychotic's experience of the collapse of any kind of temporality. Hence the focus on the question of origins and the hatred of origins, vital and revitalizing. Liliane Abensour agrees that hatred is evoked by the emptiness, the void, the reducing to nothing and the negativism that it is supposed to stand up against.

Her insistence on hatred goes hand-in-hand with the importance that she gives to the ego in the initial chapters of the book. She argues that one fundamental mechanism in psychosis is *expulsion*, with the connections between drives (*pulsion*, in French), expulsion and repulsion.

In the first chapter, there is what the reader could construe as a basic premise, that of the existence of primary narcissism. Hatred and expulsion are seen as lending support to this element. The psychotic temptation follows on from the dislocation of that basic initial situation.

Then Liliane Abensour gives up the idea of that kind of original narcissistic base. She moves away from the idea of psychosis as being a pathology only of the ego; she invites us to think of that solution as imposing itself on the ego, and perhaps even preceding it. The ego responds, she argues, to something that took place externally to it. Its dislocation is therefore a distortion. Child psychosis corroborates that point of view – with one difference: psychosis in children does not necessarily lead to psychosis in the adults they will later become.

Thus the ego and narcissism are no longer at the centre of the situation. Hatred does of course ensure that a minimum of self-preservation still exists, but it can be negativized and replaced by uncontrollable explosions of the drives and major psychical annihilations.

The psychotic patient, therefore, cannot set up any true non-temporality, since he or she is deprived of a repressed unconscious that can hold things in reserve. Such patients have either to cling very tightly to consensual temporality or to support an a-temporal "actual-ness", with no historical dimension to it, threatened by disintegration in the instantaneousness of the situation. Psychotic holding is carried out in an extemporaneous and continuous manner; no letting-go is permitted. That is why the psychotic's life is peppered with moments of collapse, withdrawal and breaking-off. It has often been pointed out that this scenario is closely related to the solution adopted by psychosomatic patients.

In Part II, the spatial axis, Liliane Abensour focuses on the topographical layout of the various inscriptions. Traditionally, the unconscious ones serve as drive representatives, while those linked to consciousness enable counter-cathexes to be carried out. Not forgetting the intermediate ones, those that are preconscious, mixed and transitional.

Towards the end of her book, Liliane Abensour takes into account a kind of inscription that she calls *liminal*; this belongs to a space between the preconscious and conscious spheres, and is a feature of writing.

The first two parts of this book combine together to offer thoughts on the manner in which the psychotic individual makes use of perceptual traces against any perception of external reality.

Part III, the most original, entitled "The Vertigo of Creation", explores how the mind generates material and how this is used in the psychotic temptation.

Drawing upon her experience of patients who had recourse to writing during their treatment and upon her knowledge of poets who have written about the experience of putting their ideas down on paper, Liliane Abensour suggests that the creation that is produced by psychosis – the delusion – takes what it needs from the *liminal* sphere, the space between Preconscious and Conscious, cut off from all contact with a regressive Unconscious. From that *liminal space* comes *liminal writing*, which fulfils several functions, a kind of writing that Liliane Abensour compares to that of poetry.

In this way, she designates a topographical locus that is specific to the psychotic solution, corresponding to a kind of writing that, following Breton and Flournoy, she calls *liminal* writing: " 'Liminal' writing is not the result of any process; it is a recourse" (*infra*, p. 117); " 'Liminal' writing is one of survival" (ibid.); "Writing can put some order into all of this and recreate (or, rather, create) a reality that remains to be defined" (ibid.); "Liminal writing has nothing to do with any process of working-through. It is an original piece of work, a pure creative impulse" (ibid.). What is specific to liminal writing and liminal reality is the fact that they are *cut off from* drive-related reality. Writing then becomes an anti-traumatic act.

The generating of neo-perceptions

Part III of the book, which deals with generating/creating, draws on another idea of Freud's: the fact that, in a psychotic situation, the task given to words is that of repairing the lack of drive-related thing-presentations, in order to self-cure, as it were, that lack.

At that point, psychical constructions are in the service of the need for certainty that is part of the self-cure. This brings us back to the connection between perception and the perceptual. The two roads to consciousness are well known: dreams and diurnal perception.

Psychical generating is then called upon to saturate the inner surface of consciousness through the use of words and images. This also maintains the dissociation between the preconscious–conscious pole and the preconscious–unconscious one.

Word-presentations lose their representative aspect; they are henceforth simply concrete signs. Pronouncing them carries with it the risk of feelings of emptiness, because of the absence of thing-presentations, and of the threat of being erased. That is when it becomes urgent to write something down – the graphical aspect of words is called upon. The materiality and the duration of writing are what are made use of; sounds are short-lived. Writing lends support to the illusion of continuity in a *locus* where no inscription or registering exists.

Identifying dreaming with a normal psychosis enables us to deduce that one of the aims of dreaming is to uphold our firm nocturnal belief that the only reality that exists is that produced by dreams. Every delusional construction must, like dreams, saturate consciousness. It is that quality of saturation which defines the perceptual element drawn from the hallucinatory dimension and which supports belief in a single reality – hence questions relating to the definition of the Real in terms of a particular aspect of perception in connection with the traumatic one of drive-extinctness. The Real dimension relates to what, in the drives, cannot be represented.

A delusion cannot be tackled head-on. The apostle Thomas's famous saying, according to which seeing is believing, is in some difficulty here. Concepts such as reality-testing and the reality principle will have to be looked at afresh. The analogy that Liliane Abensour draws with cinematography is particularly relevant here: the psychoanalyst is the "fourth wall" that enables a space for reflexivity and reality-testing.

Liliane Abensour's work is an important contribution to the theory of reality-testing. The psychotic individual tries to reduce the gap between perception and representation by asserting that conscious representation is in fact a perception, thanks to the hallucinatory solution and saturation. Operativeness diminishes that gap by eliminating representation; the neurotic does so by taking refuge in representation while simultaneously holding back any acknowledgement of a perception different from that of representation.

Liliane Abensour argues that, when there is a confrontation with reality, a disruption may occur in the person's mind. That disruption isolates him or her from the unconscious and overloads the preconscious. There then follows a kind of loop functioning in an autonomous preconscious–conscious circuit deprived of any substratum in the unconscious. The disruption changes the nature of the role of the preconscious, which becomes a kind of rampart against emptiness and nothingness – the equivalent of a protective shield against stimuli.

Cutting-off, disruption, break, "actual-ness", "out of time", "out of place" – these ideas run parallel to that of the denial of reality, the consequences of which upon the use of words and of writing I have already described. A dissociation is set up between the regressive aspects of the drives and the need for inscription/registering.

Regression is brought to a standstill. The pull of drive-related negativity can be felt through intense and nameless anxiety, catastrophic experiences, feelings of emptiness and the absence of limits, threats that know no end. The immobilization and dissociation of verbal language are psychotic responses. The perception–consciousness [Pcpt.-Cs.] system, saturated by language, is called upon to put an end to the threat of breakdown. Delusions tend to become manic and sthenic. In this way, the individual protects him- or herself through a kind of excitation aimed at abrading the negativizing internal excitation. A delusion, however, can bring in its wake major inhibitions and dislocations.

According to Liliane Abensour, it is an initial disruption that deprives the psychotic of any possibility of topographical or temporal regression. A direct relationship with nothingness, with emptiness, with the absence of limits, with blankness and fragmenting are the primary conversions experienced by psychotics; hence the constraints of decathexis, immobilization and silence. The threat is that of disappearing, being wiped out, dispersed, ejected.

The psychotic is outside of memory, of imagination, of reality, of time. "The psychotic's *modus vivendi* is characterized by the combined effect of the inability to regress, no matter in what way, and the erasing of the very notion of temporality," writes Liliane Abensour (*infra*, p. 6), who does not consider psychosis to be a state of regression. Psychotics are directly confronted with the emptiness of representation, with the emptiness of their internal object and above all with the emptiness of the psychical means that they just do not have at their disposal;[4] hence experiences of breakdown and primitive agony. Destructiveness and the compulsion to diminish are called upon to deal with these.

Liliane Abensour gives an excellent description of two systems of defence: *hyper-excitation*, with an invasion of the drives that brings in its wake distortions of the ego, and *expulsion*, in which any kind of drive-based stimulation is rejected.

The psychotic temptation and the deferred retroactive dimension (*après-coup*)

The dissociation between the two poles of the drives and the work of processing is an element that is essential for our understanding of psychosis and its treatment. That break is the most fundamental characteristic of the psychotic solution, with any processing being confined to the language pole such that there is no possibility of having an impact on the qualities of the drives. Lacan's idea of the foreclosure (repudiation) of the Name of the Father is an illustration of this.

The deferred retroactive process (*après-coup*) is the one that normally connects these two poles.

To illustrate that primary dissociation, Liliane Abensour gives the example of a drive impulse that must forever remain unprocessed. According to this view, psychosis is a deferred retroactive effect of that primary original "eruption of lava" that is non-transformable. Here a fundamental question arises: Does such a primary monism exist? Or would it be better to think in terms of a dualism that requires processing to be done in two phases?

The situation that Liliane Abensour describes can be looked upon as the first phase of the *après-coup* effect, which exists long before the second phase, that of the delusional solution, is discovered.

The content of a delusion is to be found in the same infantile world as that of the neurotic, but it has no impact on the initial traumatic phase. The major difference between the neurotic's *après-coup* and that of the psychotic's delusion lies in the fact that, in the latter, the initial traumatic phase is not modified. The reminiscences that participate in the delusion have no processing effect on the traumatic dimension that gives rise to them.

Liliane Abensour's book is a contribution to the initial phase of the *après-coup* effect, a work of research on the conditions, which, after this first phase, mean that the psychotic temptation will prevail. A delusion takes its material from a memory store and is a kind of replacement factory. However, it is because this return to how the early traumatic scene was dealt with is of no effect that any such return can only be "actual".

Liliane Abensour's theory can also be seen in terms of intra-drive splitting. There are two ways in which drive-based activity can be treated – with or without transformation of the economic aspect at its source.

The therapeutic approach

From that idea of a dislocation in the *après-coup* process derives the twofold therapeutic approach adopted by the author.

In this, Liliane Abensour makes use of the particularities of the psychotic transference, which, since it has no capacity for regression, is dominated by the compulsion to construct a neo-reality in the presence of some other person. The therapeutic set-up must take into account this transference, which is overwhelming, immediate, intense and "actual": "The here-and-now of 'actuality' is the dominant element in a space-and-time that always has to be reinvented" (*infra*, p. 115).

The author attempts to discover an appropriate correspondence between the patient's particular defence mechanisms and a technique that facilitates a therapeutic approach. She is in favour of combining individual psychoanalysis with psychoanalytic psychodrama.

What is played out in psychodrama is an attempt at encouraging the production of scenarios that promote the construction of images, which can then be used as support for remembering.

In addition, it is clear that writing may be a useful instrument in the course of individual psychoanalysis. The act of writing is a modality of inscription, the function of which is to saturate consciousness. An additional aim, however, is that of encouraging the production of regressive material thanks to the graphics of the words used.

That parallel approach to therapy rests on the hope that thing-presentations able to fulfil their role as representatives of the drives will rise out of those images. The treatment of psychotic patients requires the creation of reality-traces to make good the lack of memory-traces; that is what is required if the patient is to become able to deal with the reality of the *missing link*, that drive-based reality that remains divorced from any possibility of being represented.

Rifts in the ego

The denial that separates us from ourselves and from the world at large may at times be relatively important; it is the ever-unstable frontier between what we believe and what we refuse to believe, between what we acknowledge as true and what we imagine. How are we to take pleasure in our body without in a thousand different ways denying that it is by its very nature perishable? How are we to live if we take on board in a very clear-headed way the idea of our dying unless, more often than not, we deny that it actually might happen? How are we to move about in the world without refusing to lose ourselves in its vastness, in its boundlessness?

As human beings, we all know the paradox that consists in attempting to reconcile, to a greater or lesser extent, the denial of our body, of time and of the external world with the fundamental assertion of their reality thanks to which we exist. Psychosis arises out of that paradox; it both fascinates and frightens us because of its radical nature. The paradox that lies at the heart of psychosis has to do with the fact that, while our drives awaken desires, everything else works towards silencing them. Sexuality forms the basis for thinking that we exist; whether accepted or rejected because it both attracts and awakens fear in us, sexuality lies at the very heart of the psychotic temptation. That sexuality would like to see itself as transcended, but it is more a question of libidinal and aggressive drive impulses, arising suddenly from both inside and outside, which, given their excessive nature, their painfulness, their violence and their destructiveness, are entirely given over to trickery, short-circuits, impasses and disruptions in the ego. In a different way from what occurs in neurosis, psychosis, while being much less common, is a way of relating to oneself, to other people and to the world at large.

It can happen that, when all points of reference – temporal or spatial – have been lost, the psychotic temptation may turn into a delusional one. Breaking free of its moorings, the ego invents new continents for itself and sets up a new world order with a meaning of its own. Many patients are delusional in a quiet sort of way or sporadically; it is only after some considerable time that they will talk about their thinking, either because they do not want to feel dispossessed and faced with emptiness or because they are afraid that other people will inevitably look upon them as being mad. From that point of view, the psychoanalyst has to decide whether this is a defensive position that keeps at bay a much more invasive delusion that certain circumstances might well trigger, or whether the failure to set up a truly delusional solution (or one that comes close to it) may at times turn out to be much more damaging.

It would be unrealistic to attempt to draw up a unifying principle that would seek to define psychosis. In its widest sense, however, we can show how, as a result of drive-related impulses and their effects on the ego, the loss of spatio-temporal reference points at the crossroads between internal and external worlds opens up a whole range of psychotic possibilities; these manifestations are not in opposition to one another – indeed, they echo one another, alternate or join forces. What we must do is delimit a contextual frame that is sufficiently extensive, so that we do not fall into the trap of nosographical distinctions; it must include, as well as more obviously pathological disorders, other phases, states and modes of being. Fears, inexpressible anxieties, untimely actions, paradoxical reasoning, beliefs, words, images . . . An internal world that is more deserted than barren, as empty as it is deafening, chaotic and threatening, in which coexistence and alternation end up by merging together, in which fluctuation and temptation are synonymous.

"Limits not frontiers of psychosis?"[1] There is a vast range of ways in which people function that we include in the somewhat ambiguous category of psychosis – a range that goes from what, in the absence of any precise definition, we usually refer to as borderline states all the way to psychosis as such. What, indeed, are these limits or "borders"? The whole point, after all, is that they are vague, they are inherently mobile, they are set up only to be distorted or transformed, and they may even disappear. It is as though at the very heart of psychosis – in its widest sense and whatever form it may take – lies, not a delusion or the absence of a delusion, but an ever-present confrontation with the fundamentally unclear and enigmatic issue of understanding oneself, one's origins and the origins of the world.

In their attempts to understand psychosis, psychoanalysts have tried to define its nosographical characteristics, following more or less the psychiatric model – and this in spite of the fact that Freud's theory aimed at undermining the frontiers between normal and pathological. That is why for such a long time the only possible definition of psychosis had as its criterion the presence of a delusion or of hallucinations. This remained the case until it became clear that there were also "non-delusional" psychoses. My aim in this book is to go beyond that, but still in terms of a return to Freud's way of thinking.

Evelyne Kestemberg's experience with anorectic patients led her to the idea of what she called "cold" psychosis (1972 [1974]), one in which there is no delusion – although it has to be said that the anorectic patient's distorted body image could be likened to a kind of delusion. A first stage would no doubt be the acknowledgement of something that we find also in Herbert Rosenfeld's thinking: a "latent psychosis" (Kestemberg, 1972 [1974]) that is part of some phobic, obsessive-compulsive and psychosomatic structures. The term "cold psychosis" appears shortly after this, in 1978, in Kestemberg's paper on "The Fetishistic Object Relationship" (1978 [2001]); this led her to make certain links between classic symptomatology and Freud's metapsychology. Focusing on object relationships, Kestemberg wrote of a *delusional* dimension in which the object invades the ego and a *fetishistic* one in which there is no recourse to a delusion and the ego ideal invades the ego. In both cases, there are obstacles to free circulation between the psychical agencies. This does not in itself invalidate the psychoanalytic approach, because it constitutes above all a defensive organization that can be modified.

Evelyne Kestemberg liked to say that "cold" psychosis could turn out to be "burning-hot", given the excessiveness and massiveness of its drive-related aspect. "Cold" psychosis requires an economic and dynamic approach, one in which the transference–countertransference relationship will have to be negotiated and transformed in line with suitable modalities. What is highlighted is the way in which defences are organized in their most extreme and often combined forms, given that any object relationship is felt by the patient to be dangerous.

By contrast, as it were, "blank" psychosis, as described by Jean-Luc Donnet and André Green (1973), is based on the distinction between presence and absence of a delusion, the focus being on thinking, in an approach similar to that of Bion. ("Blank" psychosis is all too often considered – mistakenly – to be the same as Evelyne Kestemberg's "cold" psychosis [Kestemberg, 2001]; it is important not to refer indiscriminately to these two concepts.) A matrix structure conditions the possibility of psychotic development, an organization that is found in all forms of psychosis. It has two polarities: delusion when thought processes get out of control, and depression or "blank" psychosis when thinking comes under attack. The idea of structure, however – a decisive notion in the 1970s – implies a stable and lasting construction, the cohesion between its component parts being such that no one element can be dealt with or modified without taking into account those that are linked to it, because all of them will be influenced in the process. These authors argue that to a considerable extent psychosis lies outside of any psychoanalytic approach.

In the 1970s, too, Piera Aulagnier described what she called a "psychotic potentiality", a way of being that may open up the road to delusions that otherwise would remain encysted.

> By this I do not mean a latent possibility common to every subject, but an organization of the psyche that cannot but give place to manifest symptoms, and which reveals, whenever it can be analysed, the presence of a primary delusional thinking that is encysted and not repressed.
>
> (1975 [2001, p. 135])

Primary delusional thinking, in this view, is built up in an autonomous way on the basis of some defect or other, with reference to some missing meaning of or statement about origins, or in terms of one that does not follow the ordinary rules of causality. Piera Aulagnier's (1984) metaphor is that of a composite identificatory construction, in which cracks or disconnections make the overall framework insufficiently solid – a breach into which primary delusional thinking comes rushing.

Neither Piera Aulagnier nor Evelyne Kestemberg saw this situation in terms of fate or destiny. Various crossroad points or phases in life, depending on how fragile one's underlying foundations are, can determine the possible components of mental functioning with its different manifestations and developments. Faced with the threat of defusion of the drives, various arrangements can be set up that will take into account the defects and cracks that are part of the mind's construction, adapting themselves to any potential detours or negotiable bridges.

More recently, Michel de M'Uzan introduced the idea of "actual" psychosis, with its reference to psychosomatic nosography. The focus here is on the crucial principle of mentalization, the capacity to dream, to fantasize and to be delusional. In this conception, the lines of force have shifted somewhat, but the existence of two kinds of psychosis – delusional and non-delusional or "actual" – is reaffirmed. These lie on either side of an axis of meaning and self-preservation, depending on the mind's success or failure in the way in which it interprets the drives. For de M'Uzan, this new entity lies underneath the axis of meaning where "failures in mentalization, disqualification of the energy of cathexis, rejection and denial of internal reality are at work" (2005, p. 158). This again emphasizes the contrast between, on the one hand, failures and defects in thinking and, on the other, the development of a delusion, looked upon as bearing witness to a higher level of functioning even though it is of a very particular kind.

However, whether latent, potential or present, a delusion is not sufficient in itself to define psychosis (or the psychoses). Recourse to the term "non-neurotic" would probably be more relevant – but, through the use of the negative "non-", it lays emphasis on the idea of neurosis and invites us to look at the situation in its negative aspects. It would perhaps be more instructive were we to see in it a different way of being, one that remains to be discovered, highlighted and confirmed as to its specificity and originality.

It does seem possible to list the various elements that are specific to the psychoses, whether "cold", "blank" or "actual", delusional or not. The more pathological forms give us a better understanding of some kinds of functioning. This was already the case for Freud, who was able to define the mechanisms at work in the neuroses through his examination of the excesses that he found in the characteristic manifestations of the neurotic mind. We could probably do the same thing in cases of psychosis, when, in their obscure regions, they noisily reveal the distortions, disjunctions and rifts in the ego, together with the consequences that these entail.

As Evelyne Kestemberg and Piera Aulagnier have shown, there are some more or less obvious risks that arise from defects in mental organization in childhood or even before. These may entail some disorganization or other in adolescence – a time when the Oedipal situation comes once again to the fore, a period of vulnerability, when physical transformations and confrontation with the parents' sexuality (as well as with that of the individual him- or herself) disrupt the psychical equilibrium that had been set up until then. Sometimes, indeed, the impact may be traumatic, leading to severe forms of disorganization, with the threat of confusion, of breakdown or of falling to pieces. At the same time, this pattern does resolve to some extent the difficult issue of a discontinuity between infantile psychosis and its adult counterpart. The idea of childhood, of course, is not synonymous with that of the *infantile*; nonetheless, the hypothesis must be that, in psychosis, there is a disruption, either in terms of a repetition or renewal of traumatic psychical occurrences very early on in life or involving phases in which a particular kind of fragility is manifested later on.

It is important to look again at Freud's thinking about this. Taking neurotic functioning as his starting-point, and with the idea of unifying the mind and its workings, he tried to show that, in psychosis, the fundamental model of dreams and fantasy as modes of expressing repressed desires could also be found, although he acknowledged that this in itself was insufficient.

He argued that if a higher level of functioning is adversely affected, an earlier one will take over from it; this may have to be looked at afresh. For some considerable time, that way of conceiving of the situation saw psychotic patients as regressed or deprived – whereas, through their denial of their body and their exalting of some meaning that has to be found, they in fact find it extremely difficult to regress. For such patients, the road to regression remains impossible for a long time, other than through the illusion of a past which they have not appropriated for themselves, in the sense that they cannot accept it as being really their own. In the here and now of the psychoanalytic relationship, moving from "actual" to present, from emptiness or a state of merging to bodily feelings has nothing to do with having recourse to regression. The psychotic's modus vivendi is characterized by the combined effect of the inability to regress, no matter in what way, and the erasing of the very notion of temporality.

Starting with Freud's idea of the ego, faced with the pressure of the drives, being subject to distortions that may even bring about rifts, it would be helpful also to take into consideration excesses of excitation and expulsion. Sometimes these occur separately, at other times they are combined, but they always resonate with one another and are indissociable. They constitute two attempts at responding massively whenever something – whether internal or external in origin – cannot be tolerated. In his paper on "Neurosis and Psychosis", Freud (1924b [1923], pp. 152–153) says: "It will be possible for the ego to avoid a rupture in any direction by deforming itself, by submitting to encroachments on its own unity and even perhaps by effecting a cleavage or division of itself."

What I call "the psychotic temptation", without any moral or religious implication, is an attempt to express that problem situation in which, under the influence of distortions that may at times lead to a complete breakdown, deficiency and excess are linked together. This all-and/or-nothing situation is difficult to alleviate because of the threat of disorganization or falling apart when the libidinal and destructive drive impulses become traumatic and lead to an experience of chaos and of emptiness. Invasion and annihilation take hold of these patients, in whom drive-related forces are explosive, as Freud puts it in his paper "Observations on Transference-Love" (1915a [1914]).

Clinical experience supports the idea of two polarities – or, rather, of two systems of defence – that are not in opposition to each other; they are to be considered jointly, mingled together or alternating, in an approach to psychosis that is wider in scope and takes into account its gradients of intensity, when boundless excitation and evacuation go hand in hand.

When the drives become invasive, excessive excitation becomes more and more exaggerated; it distorts the ego, pushes it beyond its limits, blurs the distinction between inside and outside, between before and after – sometimes to the point of fragmentation and explosion. At that point, these patients, impervious as they are to temporality, live from moment to moment, in an insatiable and forever-unsatisfying "we want it, *now*!" By clinging to what is "actual" – and sometimes to an "action" – they find themselves beset by violence that does not come up against its object, one that knows no end-point.

In response to this – but not in opposition to it – evacuation and rejection of any kind of drive-related stimulation lead to a narrowing of limits to the point where the ego itself is erased. What then faces these individuals is emptiness, a void, a nowhere – and this may even go as far as the threat of non-existence. Such patients cling to the material, concrete world, so as not to have to face up, from the depths of their terror and withdrawal, to the vertigo and fear of annihilation.

Excessive excitation and evacuation: in response to disruptions that are more or less pronounced, more or less unfathomable, these mechanisms create situations that are "out of time" and "out of place" to a greater extent than splitting does (some forms of splitting, after all, are necessary and act as organizers).

It is the entire spatio-temporal system that is undermined when there is no continuity in the functioning of such mechanisms as processing, introjecting and internalizing. The psychotic temptation feeds on the difficulty – which is sometimes an impossibility – of having a proper base, a sufficiently solid foundation for the personality, with an infantile sexuality that corresponds to the patient's own individual and family history. It is like a book from which some chapters or pages have been removed, so that reading it leads either to confusion or to incomprehension. For some form of psychical space to be set up, for acceptable links to come together again, for temporality to play its part, a slow and patient work of weaving together is necessary – a re-structuring.

Getting back in touch with temporality and spaces in which to exist: these are two access roads, two pathways that have hardly been examined as to their theoretical implications – other than seeing them as insurmountable obstacles, whereas in fact they are full of potential discoveries if we dare to follow them in spite of their ups and downs and stretches of barren land. These two pathways require us to find markers either starting from what is actual/contemporary (in order to set up a temporal dimension that will gradually make links between past, present and future) or, when all memory traces have been erased, by opening up a space, present in its materiality and concreteness, in which traces of reality can be registered. Between two extremes, between an ego that is invaded and one that is bereft of any anchoring, bridges will have to be built and pathways opened up. References to Freud are always present, for example when he writes: "while the patient experiences it as something real and contemporary, we have to do our therapeutic work on it, which consists in a large measure in tracing it back to the past" (1914b, p. 152).

The temporal axis, which I discuss mainly in Part I of this book, looks again at the relationship between psychotic patients and registration or recording in the "Real". This at the same time calls into question the relevance of the concept of regression as regards these patients; their disorder has to do with temporality, and they are faced with confusion, emptiness and nothingness.

The spatial or material axis, discussed in Part II, proposes different kinds of anchoring. I am not referring here to what Winnicott suggested in terms of intermediate and transitional phenomena, because these have to do with different topographical and dynamic dimensions. In what I am examining, play and writing-down have as their aim either widening gaps by undoing and causing to collapse what is too firmly stuck together, or joining together, filling in and sticking together what has broken apart and become fragmented.

In Part III, I explore the vertigo of creation as a way of functioning that, lying outside of symbolizing activity as such, requires a metapsychological detour. This requires us to look again at the role of the preconscious as a kind of ferryman between consciousness and the unconscious, between past and present; I shall examine also the dissociation between words and things that is to the sole advantage of the word-part. The hypothesis that I propose is that there exists a particular area of creation that I call "liminal", lying between the preconscious and consciousness; this area is particularly well adapted to rehabilitating the kind of activity that creates verbal images, a modality that can justifiably be called "poetic".

This is not an exhaustive account but a gradual progression, a journey with some suggestions – one that is, to borrow Freud's words in a letter that he wrote to Fliess, "on the model of an imaginary walk" (1899 [1985, pp. 365–366]) through clinical experience and the reading of some key papers.

PART ONE

The Time of Psychosis: From "Actual" to "Present"

1

The question of origins

"Thanks to what I experienced and 'went through' with you," a patient said to me towards the end of her treatment, "I have the impression that I've 'paid the debt that I owed to my origins'. I feel that I've travelled over a long and difficult road to acknowledge my mother and the link that lies between us – and therefore my own existence too, and my responsibility now that I myself am a mother."

How could there be any better way of expressing the psychoanalytic trajectory which that patient followed – and it came at a heavy price – starting with the violence that weighed her down in her life, then working through her feelings of hatred until she was at last able to accept herself and her origins for what they were: after a lengthy process of identification, acknowledgment of the carnal act between her parents and of the flesh-and-blood creature who brought her into this world.

When the "origin of the world" turns out to be a woman's sexual organ, which, as in Courbet's painting, loses all its mythology and all its beliefs, it gives rise to a feeling of unease brought about not by the nakedness of the woman or her mysteriousness but by the rawness of destitution – that of the flesh, flesh that becomes either hateful or sad, as Mallarmé (1864) put it.

Depending on the modulations that are attributed to it, hate – that "sad passion", as Spinoza called it – comes in a variety of forms, whether we associate it classically with love and the ideas of ambivalence and transforming love into hate that we owe to Freud and to Melanie Klein, or with suffering, as Micheline Enriquez does (2001). It can be contrasted also with the absence of love, like the autonomous path followed by a drive impulse that, through its very violence, plays with the individual's sense of identity, life, destructiveness and death. A drive impulse at the crossroads between physical and psychical, brutal, knowing no limits – but which, paradoxically, brings the individual face-to-face with his or her own limits and may even prove overwhelming. It is precisely that aspect that has to be looked at in more detail.

For me, hating one's origins as a starting-point for thinking about psychosis evokes a powerful image related to my work as a psychoanalyst, before leading to any metapsychological considerations.

I would argue that the language of psychoanalysis, when it is properly expressed, is both a metaphorical language and a language of metaphors, as André Green has pointed out:

> Psychoanalytic discourse is focused on metaphor – I mean by that that it is not enough simply to say that it is metaphorical. Metaphor is the secret *locus* of a discourse from which everything is derived and towards which everything converges.
>
> (2003, p. 204)

Thus it is that the cosmic metaphor of light and shadow, one that can be followed through, is made use of by Freud, quite naturally, when he writes of how little we really know about the birth of sexuality. In *Beyond the Pleasure Principle*, he writes: "Science has so little to tell us about the origin of sexuality that we can liken the problem to a darkness into which not so much as a ray of a hypothesis has penetrated" (1920, p. 57).

The light of truth, as opposed to the darkness of ignorance. The same image occurs in several texts that deal with hate. Hate is a dark power, often contrasted with the brightness that is love; or again, hate as a power of evil, of darkness, contrasted with love, which is of good.

If, however, we reverse the metaphor so as to remove from it any temptation to be moral or moralistic about it, hate appears as a kind of fire, which, in turn and depending on who is involved, smoulders or bursts into flames, warms or scorches, lights up or blinds, creates or destroys.

More often than not, people are proud of their origins, but sometimes they are ashamed of them. This is because they have to deal with a primeval narcissistic problem situation, one that exists *ab initio*, one that involves "primeval origins" as the French translation puts it in "The Uncanny" (Freud, 1919 [2010], p. 126). Hatred of one's origins implies a drive impulse that threatens the individual even more, because it affects not only his or her ego but also other people. The very idea of "origins" is not at all a stable one – it is uncertain, mobile and always enigmatic, except when it is "fabricated"[1] for a period in time or in a given society, in terms of a founding myth that may be religious or even scientific. It may be harmonious, but it is just as likely to be discordant; that discrepancy may well give rise to some forms of human behaviour – the problem complex at the heart of psychosis comes from this.

Hatred with respect to origins, which can be understood as hatred *ab origine* or hatred of one's origins, is a reminder of the twofold aspect of the primeval drive-related force that is present in human beings; necessary for self-preservation and for giving the individual a solid foundation, it may also turn out to be annihilating and destructive. It is a primordial form of energy, inexhaustible, a creator both of life and of deconstruction.

Primeval hatred

As a working hypothesis that will help us in our thinking, I suggest that we begin with primeval hatred and its origins. This is the hatred, which, for Freud, lies at the very heart of the construction of the object and of the ego. In "Instincts and their Vicissitudes", Freud argues that, at a time when the object as another person is merged with the outside world, "at the very beginning, it seems, the external world, objects, and what is hated are identical" (1915c, p. 136).

At the very beginning of mental life, when the ego comes up both internally and externally against the drives, it has recourse, whenever excitation with respect to the outside world and to the object is too powerful, to a form of defence that leads to a manner of functioning in which one of two actions predominates: either the object is pushed away, or the need to attack it appears. Expulsion is therefore a primary form of reacting to unpleasure, while repelling the object is an active reaction whenever the ego experiences hatred and wants to destroy it – this may even go as far as annihilation, when hatred of the self becomes mingled with that of the other person.

We tend more often than not simply to recall Freud's statement according to which the object and what is hated are identical. Paradoxically, however, primeval hatred, given the limits that it comes up against, sets up frontiers for the ego, just as it helps in the construction of the object.

In his paper on "Instincts and their Vicissitudes", Freud, who was opposed to any kind of monism, writes: "Love and hate . . . did not arise from the cleavage of any originally common entity, but sprang from different sources, and had each its own development before the influence of the pleasure–unpleasure relation made them into opposites" (1915c, p. 138).

The idea of primeval hatred therefore helps us to see in a different light the prevalent idea of the opposition between love and hate, as well as that of ambivalence. Freud argues that their origins and functions were initially distinct from one another.

Hate in this view is a self-preservative force, one that is necessary if the ego is to survive. It represents the original "eruption of lava" as Freud put it (1915c, p. 131), the first isolated wave that will be followed by "successive eruptions" which undergo transformations, with love and hate binding together.[2]

The crucial question then becomes that of the destiny of that primary self-preservative drive, of what will become of it – the original eruption of the drive, the initial wave which does not join up with any of the others, which is not transformed; it may well be the case that it is still there, ready to be rekindled.

Through hate, the ego ties itself to the object, but drives, evacuation and repelling all follow their own path, constantly threatening the ego; in its relationship with the object, the ego always has to deal with withdrawal, emptiness and annihilation, depending on how the drives are bound together or become unbound. It is at that particular intersection that the psychotic temptation lies.

The idea of object-less violence is not as such a psychoanalytic concept; it is both a protective force related to the drives and a destructive one. It is probably useful when we explore hate in more depth, in its twofold valency of necessity and brutality, once the object can be represented.

Just as Nazism was beginning to become more prominent, Freud wrote out his reply to Einstein in a paper called "Why War?" (1933b [1932]). In it, he points out the two polarities of violence – the drive-related force, which is necessary, conforms to nature and founded in biology, and brute force, which is destructive and murderous, and which must be kept in check and deflected.

I would think it possible to apply a similar distinction to hate, even though it may seem difficult to argue that for each of these two aspects of hate – the one necessary, the other murderous – a complete transmutation of the one into the other is possible, or even that one might take precedence over the other. One kind of transformation, all the same, can take place: raw violence, with no defined object, can be transformed into hate aimed at a recognizable and recognized object.

How otherwise are we to understand the violence that the patient whom I mentioned earlier inflicted on herself through a whole series of abortions? It was as though she felt obliged, through these enactments aimed at a child but above all at herself, to offer sacrifices to some unknown, dangerous and cruel divinity. How otherwise are we to understand her giving up these destructive acts as soon as the relationship with me as her analyst began? For a long time, she thought that she could wipe out what she owed by weakening and obliterating her own ego. Unsurprisingly, any kind of Oedipal interpretation was simply brushed aside because she was unable to take it in. She felt that she was battling with a primitive mother figure, an all-powerful and terrifying Goddess with whom she could not make contact – someone who was ill-disposed towards her, someone whose anger could be warded off only through sacrifices. These sacrificial acts were a kind of conjuration through violence to keep hate at a distance. They represented also, as Freud puts it in *Totem and Taboo* (1912–1913), the most solid of links to some divinity or other, to a primeval and primary object in all of its cruelty, which lies well short of the ambivalence between love and hate. The transference relationship enabled the destructive and disruptive violence of the drives involved to be held in check insofar as the object was able to take on board the function of binding that excitation.

The risk was – and it lasted for quite some time – that, in the course of the treatment, the melancholic temptation might come to the fore, when hate turned into a "sad passion". With this particular patient, the time spent in working through melancholia was indeed long; the level of hate that attached to it was considerable. When separation and mourning are out of the question, "the shadow of the object [falls] upon the ego" (Freud, 1917b [1915], p. 249).

Poets have given the best description of melancholia perhaps because they alone know how, with words, to approach the unknown aspect of primal loss, of pain and of emptiness – the nostalgia for lost time. As Freud put it, the melancholic does not know what he has lost (1917b [1915], p. 245). The poet's oxymoron, "the black sun of melancholy" (Nerval, 1853 [1984]) expresses the paradoxical encounter between fire and shadows; when it obscures the relationship, darkness prevents the shadow, with its shape and its outline, from appearing in all of its sharpness.

On a quite different level, that of the advent of the self through the symbolic murder of the ideal child, what comes to mind is Serge Leclaire's representation of primary narcissism – a blinding light from which we have to escape in order to accede to the beneficial and delicately nuanced contrast offered by shadows. Primary narcissism, born of an original mental conception that must be put aside, encounters hate and presides "like a star, over the destiny of the child in the flesh" (p. 10). In *A Child is Being Killed* (1975 [1998, p. 3]), Leclaire writes:

> There is for everyone, always, a child to kill. The loss of a representation of fullness, of motionless *jouissance*, must be relentlessly mourned and mourned. A light must be eclipsed so it can shine and spread out on a background of darkness. Whoever does not mourn, over and over, the loss of the wonderful child he might have been remains in limbo – in the milky light of a shadowless, hopeless waiting.

Debt, murder, filiation: the death drive is present in each of these, which hate unbinds in order to set us free of the ideal that lies in each of us. It is the mother's hate for the child, mirroring her hate for her own mother and her identification with her, which by that very fact inscribes her in a line of descent.

Following Ferenczi, Winnicott – from the perspective of the primary mother–infant relationship – thought it unlikely that infants could tolerate their own feelings of hate. "He needs hate to hate. If this is true, a psychotic patient in analysis cannot be expected to tolerate his hate of the analyst unless the analyst can hate him" (1947 [1984, p. 202]). That somewhat surprising statement highlights the self-preservative and protective value of hate. Hate is also a solid link with the object, whereas violence leads to disruption, both within the self and in the relationship with the object.

Winnicott argued that the mother hates her infant even before the latter can know anything of that hate. It is therefore necessary to acknowledge the mother's hate of her child so that he or she can take it on board and process a relationship that is not restricted to that hate. Winnicott went on to list the many reasons that lead the mother (and the analyst will experience these during the treatment) to hate her infant. These go from the wound caused to the mother's body at the moment of birth to the discrepancy between the flesh-and-blood child and the idealized primary mental conception that she had of the child whom she was expecting. That discrepancy arises precisely because the child is a flesh-and-blood creature – here again, hate of the flesh.

Winnicott was describing a certain kind of regression that takes place in the course of an analysis, in which the relationship between psychoanalyst and patient mirrors that between mother and infant – the need to go back to a primary state of deprivation given the initial merging of self and object. Thanks to regression, the false self can be done away with and what had never been mentally and physically worked through can now be processed. This leads to a certain idea of psychosis – it is a regressed state linked to a primary defect. That conception of psychosis needs to be examined more closely.

Violence and the horror of one's origins

Let us look again at what Freud said: "At the very beginning, it seems, the external world, objects, and what is hated are identical" (1915c, p. 136). We shall have to decide what "at the very beginning" actually means, even though it might appear to be clear enough. *Ur*, the original, is not the beginning – and who can say what the beginning is? Even scientists, biologists or astrophysicists cannot, for they keep pushing back the date of any supposed beginning.

Unlike "primal phantasies", mentioned by Freud for the first time in 1915 in "A Case of Paranoia Running Counter to the Psycho-Analytic Theory of the Disease" (1915d), the fantasy about origins is not confined to the arbitrariness of a beginning. It invokes ancestral fears and idealizations and is expressed through myths and religions. Whatever the variations, human beings invent for themselves the beginning of their history, whether mythical or religious – the "In the beginning" that we read in *Genesis*, a story about Divinity, about Paradise, about the Fall, about rivalry, about murder . . . it is a story that in fact abolishes all notion of time and presents itself as an answer to the primary wound that the enigma of our origins always represents. Freud himself could not avoid this – he saw psychoanalysis as a theory about origins, in which the origin of the individual corresponds to that of humankind in general. In his quest for a phylogenetic explanation, Freud (in *Totem and Taboo* [1912–1913]) goes back to the prehistory of humanity, constructing the mythical story of the murder of the father of the primal horde: primeval hatred, the echo of the original violence of the group. In a similar vein, Ferenczi followed the evolutionist model and took it to the limits of its logic in his *Thalassa: A Theory of Genitality*, which contains a partly analogical, partly historical account of man and the world. A primordial catastrophe – the drying up of the land – forced the aquatic living creatures, from which human beings are descended, to adapt to sexual life and its avatars on land. Hence "this thalassal regressive trend does not cease its activity even after birth, but manifests itself in various expressions of eroticism (especially those of coitus)" (1938 [1989, p. 56]).

As we know, in his theory of seduction, Freud found it difficult to give up the idea of something that had actually occurred in childhood – "historical truth" being the basis upon which repression would be built up. According to Laplanche and Pontalis, the idea of psychical reality does, however, set some limit to imagination, which otherwise might be too unrestrained. In *Beyond the Pleasure Principle*, Freud (1920) again discussed the origin of the sexual instincts and drew the conclusion that we really know nothing about this.

The fantasy of the primeval/primal scene (*Urzene*) structures and organizes in a meaningful way the quest that an individual may set out on to understand his or her origins; it puts an end to the "infinite regression" to which unlimited questioning about origins could give rise. According to Laplanche and Pontalis (who themselves cannot avoid the issue of the origin of fantasy): "The primal scene represents for us the conjunction of the biological fact of conception and birth with the symbolic fact of filiation: it unites the 'savage act' of coitus and the existence of a mother–child–father triad" (1968, p. 11).

Through its basis in sexuality and its assertion that primal scene fantasies exist in all of us, the inventiveness of psychoanalysis is that it takes into account not only the violence of the "primal (savage) act" of coitus as the primordial origin (with its implications of castration and the difference between the sexes), but also the various impulses brought about by the hatred and the horror to which that act gives rise; the diversity of possible reactions corresponds to various kinds of functioning, whether in terms of repression or of denial.

We could say also that the question of origins, which lies at the very origin of psychoanalysis itself and puts a stop to any idea of transcendence, might well be one of the reasons for the hatred that, even nowadays, psychoanalysis comes up against.

Without question, Ferenczi – who, it will be recalled, blamed Freud for not taking into account the negative transference in the analysis that he (Ferenczi) had with him – gave the best description of the trauma that the primal scene represents for the infant, given the disparity between child and adult. Ferenczi describes the fear, disgust and hate that the infant feels, but makes no mention of anything to do with primeval hate. He concludes his paper thus: "The 'Theory of Genitality' that tries to found the 'struggle of the sexes' on phylogenesis will have to make clear this difference between the infantile-erotic gratifications and the hate-impregnated love of adult mating" (1949, p. 230).

Just as hate is part of the primal scene, the hate felt towards the primal scene and its protagonists is not out in the open as such. It makes many detours, wherever repression or denial carries it. Feeding on primal hate – the psychotic temptation is not far off – it may throw such a strong and harsh light on the primal scene that that scene becomes unbearable, to such an extent that it may give rise to feelings of terror, repulsion and horror. It could even be said that, in some ways, that hate of hate is like a fire that feeds on itself, growing stronger all the time.

When the Oedipal situation is revived, when sexual maturity brings also some realization of parental sexuality, adolescence is clearly the time when human beings are at their most vulnerable. That is why this period is a potential entry-point for psychosis.

When there is no longer any end-point represented by the primal scene fantasy, the road is open towards two poles of attraction – either towards confrontation with emptiness, with a void, or, in reaction to this, towards the creation of a neo-reality, i.e. a delusion.

Violence has to do with expelling, with expulsion, while horror – like violence, it is not strictly speaking a psychoanalytic concept – has to do with repulsion. It has a power of fascination over the ego that either paralyses it or creates such a state of excitation that the ego becomes distorted. Like violence, which is channelled through an action, horror also has a concrete and physical quality. There is a bristling about it, a shivering, feelings that are above all bodily ones. It is probably a resurgence of that primary violent and brutal drive, that first "eruption of lava", which, Freud thought, remained non-activated or at the very least autonomous; it subjects the ego to the same defence mechanisms – repulsion and expulsion – that we find in psychotic functioning.

One of my patients, plagued with questions concerning his origins – in this case, Armenian – had this to say: "I do not want to see my mother any more because what she says about filiation doesn't interest me and at the same time irritates me . . . If she's so-and-so's daughter or someone else's, it doesn't make any difference . . . It's a highly sensitive subject. Every relationship between two people is painful. It's a trap . . . It makes you lose your bearings . . . For me, sexuality has always been a threat, but I don't quite know what is threatening about it."

In this face-to-face analysis, since the patient refused to take his proper place in the maternal line of descent, I had to abide by the splitting that he set up, so that, in his quest for his origins, he would not find himself directly confronted, in a kind of short-circuit, with genocide in lieu of a primal scene. It was important to avoid any collusion between the collective trauma, represented by the systematic extermination of an ethnic group and its origins, and a primal scene fantasy – it might even have replaced that fantasy in such a way as to make it disappear.

For a long time, I found his manner of talking extremely confusing. Paradoxically, it protected him, so that he would not feel exposed to any disorganization that a too-violent and too-explosive primal scene might bring about in him. He was thereupon invaded by images that were both fascinating and exciting: a *bordel*,[3] he called it, in both senses of the word: chaos and copulation. Its violence was so destructive and disorganizing for his ego that he felt as though something was breaking its way in; that violence did not attach itself to any particular object, yet it seemed to be in all of them all of the time, giving rise to a kind of over-sexualization heavy with pornography that resulted in any attempt at constructing fantasies to fail. It was as though that violence was feeding itself, becoming an origin in the absence of any other origin.

In the foreground, there was his report of an inter-generational incest, said to have actually happened, although it did remain somewhat vague; this blocked out any possibility of remembering or working-through. The treatment was for a long time marked by silence filled with insults, alternating with abstract statements that were discarnate and hard to follow. Then another kind of silence appeared, one that he called "taking a rest from thinking", thanks to which a more coherent story could be told.

In such patients, everything works against any kind of registration in temporality; there is none of the reversibility that fantasies and memories require. Hate of origins leads to violence or persecution, although sometimes withdrawal and inhibition are uppermost. The path that we have to follow in such cases resembles the one that Winnicott took, from "Withdrawal and Regression" (1954 [1984]) to "Fear of Breakdown" (1974), i.e. to a much more complex way of looking at temporality.

On what basis can we talk of regressed patients or of regression, which is usually the case in these situations? How are we to reconcile, on the one hand, the experience of patients who, faced with a deep psychotic de-structuring, a mental catastrophe, see before them threats of a precipice and annihilation, with, on the other, the very idea of regression? They are simply not in a position to tolerate any kind of regression, be it formal, topographical or temporal.

Such patients either focus on the here-and-now "actual-ness", on some collusion between past and present – a past experience that is still present and forever being repeated – or they are cut off in a more or less decisive way from their infantile sexual history. Only the transference encounter with the analyst, whether in psychoanalytic psychotherapy or in psychodrama, can offer them enough space and create a relationship that will offer some foundation in a situation that is both primal and original – building up a new story/history, by two or more people, will take precedence over interpreting their past history.

Thanks to the analyst's mediating presence, violence is intercepted, channelled and focused. It loses some of its excessive and savage power, as well as part of the horror that accompanies it. By focusing on an object, that violence can at last be given some shape.

Denial of one's origins

Another effect of hate of one's origins, this time without excitation or confusion, is a kind of dazzling – in the strongest sense of the word – that occurs along with denial, as Paul-Claude Racamier has described so minutely (1992). The metaphor refers to the dazzling effect of a very bright light, one that blinds to the point of losing any visual scene and exposes the ego to the threat of emptiness, of loss of limits and of disappearance. With no end-point, no benchmark, no possibility of anchoring in temporality, the quest for one's origins is expressed, in a disruption and de-structuring of time, as the threat of a "before" being projected into an "after". If there is no solid foundation, there will be an endless return towards some earlier aspect, a starting-point that will never be reached, in which one is sucked up towards an absence of boundaries, towards an abstraction. It is an involution that lies on the edge of dismantling, of the vertigo of non-existence, of what has not been "created". That experience nullifies the violence of every feeling, short-circuits the materiality of the body and does away with time, as Micheline Enriquez (2001) describes. Faced with the threat of a collapse of the ego, of losing all sense of identity, the patient who is on the edge of the psychotic temptation may perhaps respond by adopting the delusional solution, often mystical or apocalyptic – it is indeed a possible solution, a way of orchestrating destructiveness, when the delusion is sufficiently well constructed. It is perhaps also a way of paying one's debt to one's origins.

A delusion is one solution to an agonizing involution that knows no end – which is not to be confused with a process of regression. Once someone has become the sole master of his or her origins, it becomes possible through a personal and original creation to set up one last organization of the self and of the world, with no before, no after (or with before and after being merged together). Even though the frontier may shift, that is where we can see the difference between, on the one hand, mythical responses that are acknowledged as such, able to be transmitted and transformed, corresponding to accepted collective options, and, on the other, the creation of a delusion the only roots of which lie in personal belief.

Contrary to mythical narratives that propose some explanation of the origins of the world and of humankind, Mary Shelley's novel, *Frankenstein*, describes the attempt by one man to produce a "creature", which, propelled by hatred because of its monstrosity and wretchedness, tries unrelentingly to destroy its creator before destroying itself.

The circumstances in which *Frankenstein* was produced are well known. One evening in 1814, in Italy, Byron, Polidori and Percy and Mary Shelley parted company after setting one another a challenge: to write a story. Mary Shelley was the only one to write a complete novel, based, she admitted, on what terrified her. At the heart of what was in fact her first novel, there is the question of origins and of creation, set out in a remarkable phantasmagoria; that aspect is all too often toned down in the many adaptations that have been made of the novel. Professor Frankenstein has the mad dream of creating a human being out of dead bodies; the result is the reality of a destructive monster. It is a matter of origins and of creation, presented, through the negation of sexuality, as a kind of subversion not only of the carnal act but also of death.

In an exemplary fashion, the novel shows just how difficult it is to set up any boundary between a legitimate question about the enigmatic origins of human beings and the mad endeavour that takes the form of an attempt at solving that riddle. Above all, in this story, we can see how difficult it is to differentiate between self-preserving hate and destructive/self-destructive violence.

Frankenstein is all of that at the same time: the product of one of Mary Shelley's harrowing dreams, it has the mad project of going back in time, of returning to things once known but since abandoned – the ideas of alchemists on transforming matter and mastering the human condition inscribed in temporality, between birth and death.

It is the filiation delusion of one man, Victor Frankenstein, who, in his hatred of sexuality and of women and with his desire to be the originator of life itself, offers a solution to the enigma of the creation of a human being. He disrupts the order of time and reverses the usual questioning about the beginning of life. Here, there is no conception and birth of a child, but the creation, from gruesome fragments, of an already-adult being – going beyond death in the merging together of death and birth. This same theme can be found in another of Mary Shelley's novels, *The Last Man*, written in 1826, in which non-existence leads to the devastation of absolute absence of existence.

It is above all in *Frankenstein* that we see this reversal of the situation that links together the creator and his creature: the hatred felt by Victor Frankenstein towards the idealized object of his creation whom he wanted to make into a "man of reason" and to whom he refused to give a partner. Somewhat paradoxically, as the monstrous creature that he has produced becomes more and more human, it expresses the loneliness and pain that it feels: "Hateful day when I received life . . . Accursed creator . . . I am solitary and abhorred." A human monster, too human, which in its hatred for its creator – who himself has become inhuman and full of hatred for his creature – will try to kill off all of those close to Victor Frankenstein before the final destruction.

The novel also expresses – therein lies the paradox – the fact that both protagonists, at one point merged together, are searching, in a Promethean or Faustian way, for something that will elevate human beings, their ambition to transcend their condition to let a new set of values come to the fore and set up new foundations for an order that is already too firmly established.

Linked to that quest, there is, for Mary Shelley, the evocation of creative literature and the anxiety that that generates when some sort of order has to be given to what is still chaotic. A necessary source of renewal and of creation, the search for our origins exposes us to the worst of illusions as well as to what is extremely destructive.

In her Introduction to the republished version of *Frankenstein* – a novel of origins par excellence, marked by Darwinism, as well as of violence and hate – Mary Shelley wrote: "Invention, it must be humbly admitted, does not consist in creating out of void, but out of chaos". Void and chaos. That is exactly the twofold danger that confronts psychotic patients; some, in their own way and insofar as they are able, try, through writing, to ward off the fear both of annihilation and of being invaded.

For psychoanalysis, over and beyond primal scene fantasies and their roots in sexuality, there remains the difficult issue of the articulation between individual aspects and group-based ones, and with it that of developments in thinking and its perversion.

The concept of origin, looked at less as a starting-point in time than as a foundation, a base on which human beings and society are constructed, has obvious flaws and weaknesses, as well as a whole range of possible fluctuations. It can be satisfactory and stable only for a given period of time or a given society or for some specific belief or other. That being the case, it includes certain elements of disharmony and disjunction between human beings and the world – when "the time is out of joint", to borrow Hamlet's expression from the depths of his melancholy.

These disjunctions enable the eruptions of lava to explode once more – that constant force, an integral part, because of its permanent nature, of self-preservation – in acts of physical violence, in which brutality and horror play a major role.

"Why War?" asked Freud. War – or, even worse, massacres and genocides – carried out in the name of an ideology of origins, whether the excessive or abusive assertion of one's own origins and those of one's compatriots or the sweeping denial of those of other people.

This is the closed circle of hate and destructive violence. At this crossroads between the individual and the group, between the physical and mental dimensions, between acts and delusions, the enigma of origins, by its very instability and the always provisional and partial answers that are offered, is to some extent connected to the existence of disruptions and deficiencies.

2

When going back is impossible

Something that Freud said is crucial for our understanding of why, in patients whose mental organization is psychotic, time seems to slip by or, even more often, to come to a halt. Under the influence of powerful drive impulses, set in motion by internal or external sources, the ego is subjected to psychical distortions that may lead to break-ups. In "Neurosis and Psychosis" (1924b [1923]), Freud wrote:

> it will be possible for the ego to avoid a rupture in any direction by deforming itself, by submitting to encroachments on its own unity and even perhaps by effecting a cleavage or division of itself. In this way the inconsistencies, eccentricities and follies of men would appear in a similar light to their sexual perversions, through the acceptance of which they spare themselves repressions.
>
> (pp. 152–153)

Later, as he continued to explore in depth the question of psychosis, he used the word "rift" – a more colourful image, perhaps, and certainly one that is more violent and far-reaching than his earlier description of the ego being disrupted by what he called cleavage. This corresponds to an extreme situation in the conflict that opposes drive-related demands and reality: "a rift in the ego which never heals but which increases as time goes by" (1940b [1938], p. 276). It is not difficult, therefore, to understand why the ego's temporal frontiers are lost, whenever such a flaw occurs – and even more so in the case of a disruption.

When I asked one of my patients what he was feeling, he replied that he did not know what to say because he did not understand what part of himself I was talking to. What he meant by that was not that there were two split-off parts of himself that existed simultaneously and which took turns in manifesting themselves, but that there was what he called a "disruption", a "break" that prevented him from having access to how he was and to what he felt before that rift occurred. He found himself either facing an insurmountable wall, an impasse, or on the other side of a wall that had crumbled. He then felt lost, in a kind of free-fall, or at times in a virtual world from which there was no escape. It was only after a long and patient work of weaving things together in the here-and-now relationship with the analyst that he could get back in touch with himself and with his past – a past that was traumatic or at least experienced as such. The difficulty lay in the fact that it was impossible for him to take stock of himself; his present situation was painful, given that he felt overwhelmed by incestuous ideas and threatened by a void that opened up in front of him, a substitute for the past that was for him inaccessible.

In such circumstances, any "disruption" represents a significant moment, one that may be precisely timed. It takes on the appearance of an inaugural moment, as if everything began at that particular instant; anything that occurred earlier is wiped out and denied. The fault lines in psychotic patients have to do with the impossibility in which they find themselves of inscribing their past within a temporal experience, as if any kind of retroactive functioning were excluded.

How are we to reconcile such phenomena as a more or less pronounced fragmentation and shattering of the ego, cracks that may be very deep, with the idea of regression – topographical, formal or temporal – that is part of the classic form of psychoanalytic treatment? It is still often said that psychotic patients are regressed. But is there really in such patients any attraction or pull towards a timeless unconscious? We must not mistake the timeless nature of the unconscious for the absence of time – or, rather, the exit from time – that is typical of psychosis, with its way of evading the temporality of past, present and future, the vector of life that is an integral part of the way in which our thinking can go back and forward.

Freud described mental functioning as being in two phases, which are very different depending on whether that functioning is neurotic or psychotic in nature. It may therefore be necessary to re-examine, in addition to the relationship with reality, the idea of regression as well as that of psychical causality, which is closely linked to it.

The two phases of mental functioning

After the turning-point that was 1920 and his structural theory, Freud explored psychotic functioning, focusing on the idea of reality. While seeing the id as a reservoir of the drives in both neurosis and psychosis, Freud described the existence of a frontier between two situations: in the one, the ego is struggling against the id and swears allegiance to the outside world, while in the other, the ego is dominated by the id and de-cathects the external world. In psychosis, therefore, the conflict is between the ego and the external world, while in neurosis the conflict is between the ego and the id. In psychotic patients, the ego is therefore caught between two equally threatening poles – the id and external reality – and becomes distorted. This gives rise also, inter alia, to distortions in the perception of time.

It is noteworthy that Freud's comparison between neurosis and psychosis led him, in each case, to conceive of mechanisms that operate in two phases and in opposite directions. In neurosis, the first phase consists in repressing a fragment of the id or drive-impulses, while the second phase is a flight from reality and the return, in a regressive movement, to fantasy life; fantasies, he went on to say, are backed up by reality. In psychosis, the first phase starts with reality. Here, the mechanism is one of denial, not repression. In the second phase, a neo-reality is constructed, in which a fantasy world replaces external reality. From the outset, then, the two phases involve different topographical categories – repression is linked to the unconscious, whereas denial operates on reality, on consciousness. In addition, with repression and negation on the one hand and denial and splitting on the other, these mechanisms stand in stark contrast to one another: in neurosis, reality (or a part of reality), whether external or psychical, is not rejected – it is avoided, circumvented; in psychosis, it is blocked off and denied, and a neo-reality is created as a substitute for it.

Many factors led Freud to think deeply about the composition of the fantasy world which, in psychosis, leads to this neo-reality, "the store-house from which the materials or the pattern of building the new reality are derived" (1924a, p. 187). What, indeed, is the content of this neo-reality? Is it the same as in the neuroses, so that it can be rediscovered through regression and the lifting of repression? Is fantasy in the narrow sense of the word the proper term to use here? How does the substitution come about? What mechanism is involved?

In spite of his attempts to reconcile the two in his comparison between neurosis and psychosis, Freud concludes his paper on "The Loss of Reality in Neurosis and Psychosis" in this way: "Thus we see that both in neurosis and psychosis there comes into consideration the question not only of a *loss of reality* but also of a *substitute for reality* (1924a, p. 187, italics in the original).

Later, in *An Outline of Psycho-Analysis* (1940a [1938]), the picture that Freud paints of the situation is more complex; he goes back to the distinction between internal and external that he had drawn in "Instincts and Their Vicissitudes" (1915c) and says:

> This tallies very well with what we learn from clinical experience – namely, that the precipitating cause of the outbreak of a psychosis is either that reality has become intolerably painful or that the instincts have become extraordinarily intensified – both of which, in view of the rival claims made on the ego by the id and the external world, must lead to the same result.
>
> (1940a [1938], p. 201)

Freud's thinking on these issues did change, all through his attempts to clarify what took place. He was sorely tempted to see psychosis as part of a general pattern, in which the psychotic patient's manner of being – and the delusional aspects involved in this – would come from a common source, whatever the distortions; this would be similar to what he called "a picture of the patient's forgotten years" (Freud, 1937, p. 258).

In that paper ("Constructions in Analysis"), after describing the two stages (the two phases) of psychoanalytic treatment – the transference relationship and forgotten elements of the patient's childhood – Freud shows how the preliminary work of construction, based on the patient's dreams and free associations, can open up a path that enables memory traces to emerge, thus reinforcing the patient's adhesion to the treatment process. The fact that some of these memories have a hallucinatory aspect led Freud to draw a parallel between these and the delusional productions of psychotic patients; he saw in these – in a way similar to dreams, but in a more distorted and indirect manner – the fulfilment of a wish subjected to the force of the repressed. "In this way a proposition which I originally asserted only of hysteria would apply also to delusions – namely, that those who are subject to them are suffering from their own reminiscences" (1937, p. 268). We could therefore say that underneath the delusion there is always some degree of "historical truth" that has to be revealed to the patient in order to bring him or her back to the event in the past, the part of reality that had been denied. A delusional belief, in this view, would have its source in a similarly strong belief dating from the patient's childhood.

It is true that, for Freud, all human beings could develop delusions, the historical truth of which lies in the repression of a forgotten time going back to their origins. We must, however, remember that he did have reservations about any attempts to treat repression and denial as more or less the same; indeed, he emphasized the difference between them: "It will be the task of each individual investigation to reveal the intimate connections between the material of the present disavowal and that of the original repression" (1937, p. 268). Here again, Freud's thinking moves forward a step at a time. Given that, it would perhaps be wiser to see in a different light the "material" that lies at the heart of psychosis. In a way similar to Freud's notion that hysterics suffer from reminiscences, we could perhaps say that psychotic patients can be described – not necessarily defined – as "suffering from temporality".

Their temporality is altered in many ways that are distinguishable from the complex mechanisms of repression and of alternation between remembering and forgetting, between continuity and discontinuity: a distorted temporality in which stasis and disruption play their part. This significantly modifies, for psychosis, Freud's model of dreams and fantasy life as found in the neuroses.

That is indeed the issue that any clinical treatment of such patients has to deal with: for these patients, recalling their past history, whether real or fantasized, is more often than not impossible, either because it is too exciting and too painful (and therefore traumatic), or because the breaks that occur in it are too much of an obstacle. Any relationship to the past, to memory, to time is blocked, paralysed or broken off; this is an indication of another way of functioning that is not just the absence of temporality, as though reality and temporality could simultaneously be abolished. Some element of reality and of temporality still remains.

Here, the important issue is that of the validity or otherwise of the notion of the deferred retroactive effect (*après-coup*) – a concept that is particularly significant in the neuroses – and of the two phases of psychical causality that derive from it. Freud first mentions it in his "Project", but develops it much more fully in his study of the "Wolf Man" (1918 [1914]) case history. The concept of *après-coup* implies that mental processes can be both retrogressive and progressive. In the classic form of treatment, it has to do with the lifting of repression and a possible access to a temporal phase linked to primal fantasies that become meaningful only in the second phase. This is a complex kind of temporality, one that runs counter to determinism; in psychoanalytic treatment, it is revealed or confirmed, thereby enabling earlier experiences to be processed. This is not simply a matter of "deferred effect", as it has sometimes been translated; there is also a "retroactive impact" – a time interval that makes meaningful something that has in fact already occurred.

As I have pointed out, with psychotic patients, however, it is difficult – and sometimes impossible – to go back to a past experience. In such patients, disturbances of the ego and of temporality are such that a more appropriate approach is required. The ego is at times locked in a time frame that is suspended and immobile, one in which past and present are all mixed up; time may be fragmented or diffracted, or still constantly expanding until it becomes unlimited. The very notion of time, in these patients, has been abolished.

The dangers of regression

How, then, are we to bring together, on the one hand, the mechanisms of denial and splitting – or perhaps it would be better to say the impact of the rifts that are so powerful in psychotic functioning – and, on the other, the idea of regression? What is implied here is a topographical and formal difference. It is hardly likely – the hypothesis at any rate is not particularly convincing – that there exists a psychotic ego, which, thanks to some form of regression, would be able to go back to earlier phases of the development of thinking and of object relations – all the way back, in fact, to a primary phase of omnipotence, completely dominated by the pleasure principle. We are no longer at the point where, as Laplanche and Pontalis (1973, p. 388) put it somewhat derisively: "it is sometimes said of the schizophrenic that he turns back into a baby at the breast, or of the catatonic that he returns to the foetal state."

It was no doubt the introduction of the concept of the death drive in 1920 that – wrongly, as it happens – lent weight to the idea that psychotic patients are regressed. The argument was that, faced with the risk of destructiveness, the ego could have recourse to regression, which might go as far as returning to a primary an-objectal phase. The hypothesis of primeval repression reinforces that idea, the melting-pot that is the id being common to both neurosis and psychosis, as described by Freud. That primeval source and the mystery that surrounds it were the starting-point for thinking about new conceptions of psychosis by some of Freud's successors – Melanie Klein, Piera Aulagnier and Wilfred Bion in particular. Taking as their basis a primitive and primeval pattern of functioning, several analysts have tried to draw nearer to that zone at the beginning of time, the *primum movens* from which human beings emerged, where the risk of failings and disruptions is all too present – their resurgence comes about because secondary repression is out of the question. In this view, the violence of psychosis directly involves primary drive impulses; indeed, it is no more than a manifestation of these. The cohesiveness of this theory must not, however, make us lose sight of just how difficult, clinically speaking, it is for psychotic patients, deprived of any elements of causality, to overcome the chaos and avoid the disorganization that any kind of regression in reality would only amplify were it to be attempted.

Freud's initial intuition as to regression can be found in his "Project". He makes use of a metaphor to describe it: "a stream of water which meets with an obstacle is dammed up and flows back into old channels which had formerly seemed fated to run dry" (1950 [1895], p. 345). The spatial image of a river, of the road that life follows, is indeed a representation of the classic temporal vision that we have of human development.

Although dreams may be the perfect model for regression and open up the road to an understanding of the unconscious, Freud's description of regression does all the same lend itself to confusion: at times part of his metapsychological conception, at others it is simply a description of a defence mechanism. The three forms that regression may take – topographical, formal and temporal – are most of the time looked upon as belonging to the same pattern. "All these three kinds of regression are, however, one at bottom and occur together as a rule; for what is older in time is more primitive in form and in psychical topography lies nearer to the perceptual end" (1900, p. 548). As he argued in the "Dora" case (1905c [1901]), pathology implies a return to an earlier phase of human development.

In chapter 7 of *The Interpretation of Dreams*, topographical regression is described as a retrogressive movement of excitation towards the perceptual pole; temporal regression is, nonetheless, the main factor. It is this that makes for a return towards earlier kinds of functioning that are less structured or less differentiated, in a reverse-direction genetic sequence drawn towards the perceptual pole.[1]

To this was added, in *Three Essays on the Theory of Sexuality* (Freud, 1905b), the idea of fixation – points at which something is registered, making for a possible halt in the retrogressive or backward-moving process. Which, then, takes precedence over the other? Which comes first – regression or fixation? Are those points necessary so that what is therein registered can be brought into play, or are they above all defensive? The issue of precedence in time is always a crucial one.

Freud went on, in his "A Metapsychological Supplement to the Theory of Dreams" (1917a [1915]), to differentiate between two kinds of temporal regression: one of them affects the development of the ego, with a return to an earlier way of functioning, while the other involves the libido and a return to the libidinal object. A little further on, he argues that regression per se is not a metapsychological concept, contrary to what he had earlier thought: "We cannot tell where we should localize [regression] in the mental apparatus . . . [it] is a purely descriptive [notion]" (1916–1917 [1915–1917], p. 342).

It is probably the case that, as regards psychotic patients, there has been some confusion between, on the one hand, exploding and fragmenting, becoming merged and paradoxical thinking, and, on the other, the primary processes of displacement, condensation and non-contradiction. The mistake seems to have been to think of psychotic patients as regressed or deprived – a mistake that led along the wrong track. It also used to be said that psychotic patients did not dream, whereas what they find difficult is not that they are unable to dream but that they cannot easily differentiate between dreaming and reality; the mere narrative of a dream then often becomes terrifying, as is the fact of going back to something too exciting which happened in the past and which again becomes accessible.

Regression, which cannot be dissociated from its accompanying forward-directed movement, is not only possible but also necessary in the treatment of neurotic patients, with its links to the lifting of repression. That path, however, as Bion pointed out – I shall come back to this later – is not open to patients who function in a psychotic manner, i.e. those who are subject to some disturbance of temporality or perhaps even to the suspension, albeit partial, of all temporal vectors. There is no way back; if there were one, it would be fraught with threats of exploding, fragmenting and falling apart. The mechanisms by which such patients defend themselves against the danger represented by any confrontation with their drive impulses or object relations at different phases in their life have their own particular characteristics that determine how they operate.

Federn understood that particularly well. He argued that, even in the classic form of analysis, given the regression that it implies, there is a significant risk of awakening some latent psychosis or other. He was all in favour of certain technical modifications in the analysis of psychotic patients, while insisting on the fact that these did not amount simply to psychotherapy based on a superficial knowledge of psychoanalysis. He argued that, "In psychoses, the same method means the opening of dams and sluices during inundation" (1952, p. 135). The difference in method lies in the handling of resistance and of the transference. Free association and the analysis of the transference should be put aside; explanations should be given to the patient as regards his or her way of functioning. Federn put it quite clearly when he said that, "*in neuroses, we want to lift repression; in psychoses, we want to create re-repression*" (1952, p. 136).

Federn quite obviously saw the danger to which regression gives rise, but his conception of the unconscious remained that of something that was too exposed and had to be encapsulated. Faithful to Freud's teachings, the model that he had in mind was that of the neuroses. His basic premise was that there was some defect or other, a disorder that must not be allowed to emerge. It is true that, for as long as is necessary, we must give up any idea of a process based on a return to primary mechanisms in the service of the pleasure principle; we must nevertheless take into account and go along with the specific defence mechanisms that are an integral part of distortions of the ego in situations in which denial, splitting and projection are uppermost, in a gradual attempt to subvert them, as Evelyne Kestemberg put it so graphically (2001). The aim of these distortions, as Freud pointed out, is to avoid any disruptions; these, however, cannot always be avoided, and they may take many forms.

These disruptions are always a threat. They are in contradiction not only with the process of repression but also with any progressive or retrogressive movement in fantasy life, "a more satisfying real past", as Freud wrote (1924a, p. 187), or an unsatisfying one that therefore has to be modified, as Winnicott put it. Given the mechanisms of denial and splitting, as well as the rifts that may occur, the construction of a neo-reality is of necessity cut off from any accessible foundation, from any possibility of processing based on something that lends itself to interpretation. From the very outset, the difference is indeed topographical.

Winnicott was very much in favour of regression in the course of psychoanalytic treatment, especially in the case of psychotic patients. He contrasted this with the kind of withdrawal that they tend to adopt in order to avoid distressing experiences, with the aim of preserving their ego. In such cases, Winnicott argued, there is a disregard for reality, a feeling of unreality that, to his way of thinking, impeded the necessary regression. There is a continuum that, from a developmental point of view, goes from biological drive to the mature stage of emotional development; he defined regression as "simply . . . the reverse of progress" (1954 [1984, p. 280]), adding a little further on that this is not a "simple reversal" but "the existence of an ego organization and a threat of chaos" (p. 281).

In Winnicott's view, the false self that these patients set up from an early phase of deficiency in their life or of some failure impossible to overcome represents a part of the ego that develops in parallel with the true self, that remains hidden and paralysed. These two modalities of being coexist; they need to be re-harmonized through recourse to regression. This can occur, he argues, only if the patient becomes aware of the deficiency in the environment that was earlier experienced and is now being re-experienced in the transference.

This regression is therefore more narcissistic than drive-related; that is why it does not entail the deadly disorganizing aspect that regression may take on. This reminds us of what Freud called "the patient's forgotten years" (Freud, 1937, p. 258) in the grip of suffering, fear and deficiencies much more than of drive-related violence. For Winnicott, there are two kinds of regression. In the one, there is a return to a situation of primary environmental failure that may provoke anger against such situations and thereby lead to their unfreezing; in the other, there is a return to a situation of dependence and of adaptation to the environment that continues to the stage of primary narcissism.

Putting the analyst in the position of a good-enough mother, as Winnicott does, immediately locates the origin of psychosis in early infancy, at a stage when there is no anchoring as yet in space and time. The psychoanalytic situation then becomes a reparatory analogon to the mother–environment–infant relationship. That is why it is important to create dependence. To the failure in the progressive outlook corresponds the need for a retrogressive movement, so as to create environmental conditions that will facilitate the development of a true self. It also attributes to a specific causal factor or factors something which, in the mental life of these patients, hardly ever shows itself in such a deterministic light.

How are we to understand Winnicott's apparently contradictory statement according to which a patient may recover spontaneously from psychosis? "Psychosis is closely related to health, in which innumerable environmental failure situations are frozen but are reached and unfrozen by the various healing phenomena of ordinary life, namely friendships, nursing during physical illness, poetry, etc., etc. " (1954 [1984, p. 284]). Strangely enough, we could perhaps see in these healing processes a specific relationship to temporality, a kind of immediacy that corresponds to the particular nature of psychotic patients, much more than a capacity for regression. The point is to offer them a presence, something that, having once existed, has been lost – as we shall see later – something that may reappear or be (re)created through a relationship with other people, with their own physical body, with writing.

Here, Winnicott's mentioning of the recourse to poetry seems to me to be of special value, insofar as poetry, through its very economy of means, defies not only interpretation or logical progression but also temporal unfolding. When poetry arises, it is a revelation, the art of the moment.

This leads to the question of psychical causality and how we can understand it in relationship to a form of temporality that is turned upside-down, paralysed or perhaps even abolished altogether.

Psychical causality and temporality

Some twenty years later, in a major article called "Fear of Breakdown" (1974), Winnicott described his new understanding of psychosis, taking into account the risk of deficiencies in the ego's defensive structure and the threat of breakdown in the establishment of the unit self.

Winnicott's basic thesis is that breakdown has already taken place in the patient at a point in time when he or she was not really able to experience it as such; Bion would take up this idea, in a different way, in terms of projective identification. This leads again to the question of temporality and regression, with respect to a psychical causality that occurs in two phases. This time, these two phases do not coincide with the two phases of Freud's deferred retroactive impact (*après-coup*); but they make meaningful a past event which, although it did actually take place, could not be properly experienced or registered in memory because the ego was not at that point sufficiently mature. Winnicott emphasizes the primeval nature of these experiences. His hypothesis is that of a continuum determined at birth – or perhaps even before birth – by an environment that is more or less "facilitating". That continuum protects the self from the unconscious, the locus of every danger, which could otherwise give rise to the risk of non-integration, of loss of the sense of reality or of some "failure of indwelling".

The clinical picture that Winnicott paints based on what he calls "primitive agonies"[2] is indeed the one that we encounter in our work with psychotic patients. What they talk to us about most of the time is their fear of annihilation, of emptiness, of non-existence. The word *breakdown* is evocative of two images – a collapse and a stoppage. Here we have the combined impression of disintegration and of the paralysis that attempts to prevent it from taking place. Winnicott emphasizes the ambiguity that surrounds these anxieties, which are simultaneously dreaded and compulsively sought out. He sees in them a twofold characteristic: they have first to be experienced and only then set up as defensive modalities. In contrast to Federn, Winnicott argues that it is not possible to do without that experience in the course of an analysis; it is that element which ensures, in a way similar to remembering, that what had never really been felt can henceforth be experienced as such.

For Winnicott, the origin of psychosis does indeed lie in the individual's early infancy; some failure or other in the environment has an impact on a phase that precedes any spatio-temporal anchoring, a phase that cannot be thought about and remains inaccessible. That experience, however, must be brought into the here-and-now of the analysis, lived through as a primary experience that belongs to the past at the same time as it presents itself as a projection into the future.

Winnicott does point out that his conception of the unconscious is neither that of Freud nor that of Jung. "In this special context, the unconscious means that the ego integration is not able to encompass something" (1974, p. 104). It is, for him, a primary experience that could be called pre-unconscious. It still has to do with regression, but in a provisionally suspended temporality, where the timeless nature of the unconscious merges with the hampered temporality of psychotic patients. There is still the idea of a reversal of the process of maturation in human development – so that the retrogressive movement is still very much a feature – but the picture that Winnicott now paints is much more complex and much closer to our clinical experience with psychotic patients.

It is a strange way of putting it, yet it is convincing: what has to be shown to the patient is something that he or she has experienced without really feeling it. These two phases are quite different from those of the deferred retroactive effect, in which the second phase, given the denial and splitting necessary to shore up the ego, cannot easily be connected to the first one; it is as though that first phase was still at work, without any possible recourse, contrary to the action of repression and its lifting. Does this first phase, marked by the ego's immaturity, bear witness to a failure of primary repression and deficiencies in auto-eroticism?

As Winnicott himself puts it:

> It must be asked here: why does the patient go on being worried by this that belongs to the past? The answer must be that the original experience of primitive agony cannot get into the past tense unless the ego can first gather it into its own present time experience and into omnipotent control now.
>
> (1974, p. 105)

This more complex picture of temporality brings to mind Piera Aulagnier's description of a primeval phase that, being elusive, may, in people who present a particular kind of fragility, lead to a "psychotic potentiality".

The threat of defusion may emerge between point #0 at birth – a "before-ness", an already-there of the body and its needs that one must be able to think about – and point #1 – access to the "I", the first-person dimension, in a process of identification, when the possibilities of one's mental functioning are established. To counter that threat, idealization and self-prohibition are the preferred defensive modalities. That originary element provides a special function, that of containing as distinct from registering memory traces that can later be recovered and repeated; here, however, the danger involved in untimely interpretations appears in all of its violence. For Piera Aulagnier, the idea of psychical causality, when psychosis appears on the scene, leaves room for a random aspect (Aulagnier 1984), but the fundamental cause appears when the speaker's words do not match the shared discourse.

It would certainly be possible to place more emphasis on the enigmatic quality of the self and of the world in psychosis, and to generalize the mismatch between self and object, given the rift in the ego, the lack of understanding, the constant discrepancy, the disharmony that follows on from it and constitutes the fundamental enigma. What then happens is that the individual is obliged to construct an inappropriate kind of causality divorced from all desire, from all memory. We could say that the blurring of any relationship of causality is one of the hallmarks of psychosis.

In bringing together desire and memory, Bion undoubtedly showed how the psychotic patient, faced with his or her intolerance of the depressive position, with internal persecutions and with those of verbal thinking so closely linked to catastrophe and pain, finds it both impossible to go back to an inner state of being and too difficult to go on with verbal thinking. The only available recourse is projective identification, a substitute for repression; the analyst has to show this to the patient so as to encourage some awareness of his or her psychical reality. According to Bion, memory and desire follow two contrasting pathways. "Memory and desire may be regarded as past and future 'senses' (analogous to the mathematical concept of 'sense' and applying indifferently to time or space) of the same 'thing'" (1967 [1984, pp. 143–144]). To highlight the impasse, or perhaps the only solutions possible when faced with these contradictory movements, he goes on:

> Making use of sense in this way a formulation $\overleftarrow{\text{desire}}$ would have the same value as $\overrightarrow{\text{memory}}$, the former referring to an event that had happened and the latter referring to an event that had not happened and therefore not usually described as being "remembered".
>
> (p. 144)

Here the second phase gives a somewhat different meaning to the idea of construction from that which Freud envisaged, based on mechanisms of burying and forgetting (the archaeological comparison) because it takes loss and destruction into account.

Several of these issues will influence our practice as analysts, depending on whether we focus more on the origin of disorder or on the defensive patterns that can be observed. Two theoretical and clinical itineraries thus present themselves to us: in the one, we may take as our starting-point the idea of a deficiency, of an original something that is lacking, something that the patient must re-experience in the course of the treatment for a better distribution of his or her cathexes of object relations to be implemented; in the second, given the sheer weight of the splitting or disruptions that are at work relative to the life of the drives in the patient, we may well think that it will take some considerable time before we can rely on regression, whether we see this as a return to an earlier state or, as Bion suggests, a return to an internal state. Other approaches will have to be found, ones that enable transitions and pathways to be set up with the aim of diminishing these rifts.

The threat of breakdown is a particular kind of experience that has nothing to do with a process. It is a risk, and also a temptation – that of rushing headlong, of being sucked in, of excruciatingly imploding. The struggle against fears of annihilation, of emptiness, of non-existence means going through a phase of paralysis or clinging to what is "actual" – not in terms of a temporal aspect that could take on a dimension of duration or length of time, like "the present", which, no matter how fleeting and short-lived, is linked both to the past and the future, but as something here-and-now, immediate, bereft of all anchorage.

The dreaded moments when the ego collapses and breaks down suddenly appear in a shattering way, almost always at a time when there is an encounter between the drives and the reality of sexuality acted out or about to be enacted – at the end of adolescence, for example, that particularly vulnerable phase in which the ego and parental imagos are being modified. Psychosis in its different forms, delusional or not, often begins at that stage in life; but it is only this second phase, that of the encounter with sexuality, cut off from an initial phase that is badly structured or perhaps not structured at all, which can be taken into account by the psychoanalyst.

Patients who function in psychotic mode live in a category of time that is in complete confusion. There are no markers, so that they never experience the retrogressive and progressive movements that allow some degree of circulation between different times and different psychical agencies. They are stuck in the immediate "actual-ness". The other possibility is that, without any fixed markers or point of origin, they may well risk involution – not regression – rushing headlong towards something that they can feel to be an abyss, a chasm. Worse than that: the disruption of temporality leads them to think that the precipice may just as well be in front of them – when it takes the form of a premonition of catastrophe – as behind them, as Winnicott (1974) described it in "Fear of Breakdown", i.e. something that has already occurred but was never really experienced.

Without being able to take any support from past experience, caught in the grip of the enigma of their existence, some have no other way out than to lose themselves in the enigma itself, in emptiness and confusion. They may also, perhaps, attempt to solve – mistakenly – the mystery by adhering to a delusional construction as a kind of psychical causality that is both unyielding and leads to confusion. The threat of collapse or of breakdown that weighs on their ego means that psychotic patients lose all access to their primeval fantasy world; they sometimes have to have recourse to a delusion as a way of explaining the world, of creating a new reality. Similar breakdowns and collapses can be found in extreme situations, when the individual is faced with an unbearable reality that can neither be avoided nor transformed. Incest and the concentration camps are two such examples; as we know, they may well trigger psychotic ways of functioning.

3

"Actual-ness", broken time, time in confusion

In *An Outline of Psycho-Analysis*, after pointing out that excitation can come from the internal as well as from the external world, Freud goes on to say: "The problem of psychoses would be simple and perspicuous if the ego's detachment from reality could be carried through completely. But that seems to happen only rarely or perhaps never" (1940a [1938], p. 201).

When excitation is prevented from being transformed into a bearable kind of drive-related energy, it becomes traumatic and the links between internal and external reality become blurred and begin to unravel. Basically, psychosis is perhaps a way of questioning reality rather than negating it; certainly, because of that, it takes on an enigmatic quality. The classic form of psychoanalytic treatment does not directly address issues that concern external reality or at least sees them as less important than psychical reality; it therefore does not take on board this faltering of the ego, this disjunctive effect which destroys links and which is always part of any challenge to external reality, given the threat that it might disappear and lead to breakdown. That threat is so powerful in psychotic patients that it defines their relationship to time within such an upheaval and, more generally, their way of being as regards themselves and the world at large.

In his paper on "Negation", Freud (1925c) links the idea of judgement to primary drive impulses. At the origin of defusion of the drives, what is good is introjected into the pleasure-ego while anything bad is excluded. What he calls "the negativism which is displayed by some psychotics" (1925c, p. 239) – i.e. their destructiveness – is "probably to be regarded as a sign of a defusion of instincts that has taken place through a withdrawal of the libidinal components" (ibid.). The other component of the intellectual function of judgement, which, says Freud, decides whether or not something that is represented actually exists, should perhaps be taken even more into consideration. This has to do with the reality-ego and consists in deciding whether something that takes the form of a representation in the ego may or may not also be perceived.

Magritte's paintings are a good illustration of this because they call into question the way in which we see the world. "This is not a pipe" says one of them in very careful writing – and in so doing creates a feeling of unease that involves the presence of the representation of an object together with its verbal negation. The treachery (or treason) of images, indeed, because it places us in a paradoxical situation: the object is represented, yet at the same time its very existence is called into question. We can accept the truthfulness of a statement referring to the actual and concrete reality of a pipe – the painting, with its pictorial representation, is not, of course, a pipe. As often occurs with Magritte's word-paintings, the fit between an object and its name or even a designation standing in for the object can leave us in doubt. Over and beyond all that, is there not some calling into question of reality itself? Given the disruption between visual sensation and mental process, there is somewhere the paradoxical idea of something that we should accept as simultaneously existing and not existing.

When the disruptive discharge of drive energy leads to a distortion of the ego – and sometimes to a disruption between the ego and internal reality, with no link possible between them – external reality is experienced as a traumatic event because of its overwhelming intensity and of the drive-related violence that it triggers. It bursts into the ego and makes the concrete nature and meaning of perception falter, in circumstances where perception ought to provide a solid basis. Psychotic patients then cannot get in touch with their perceptions, hence the deep sense of disturbance that they feel, and they find themselves in the grip of doubt. Their only way out is to cling to what lies in the here-and-now of "actuality".

Reality and temporality

What, then, happens if something from outside, something belonging to external reality, cannot be symbolized? How are we to understand the obstinate insistence – sometimes awkward – with which some patients want us to acknowledge the concrete reality of what they have experienced? What comes to mind here is the firm belief that Freud had, before he abandoned his *neurotica*, concerning the reality of the seduction scenes about which his patients told him. We may, all the same, be underestimating the importance of the ambiguity of external reality – a threat, but also a means of reassurance.

It often happens that reports involving external reality – sexual abuse, incest or particularly stressful situations – cut off all access to fantasy and to any kind of symbolization; yet the patient is looking for some reassurance as regards the reality of what he or she experienced and the firm belief that arises from it. It is as though a "real" traumatic event, which intervenes not as a screen but as an obstacle to any working-through, had to be confirmed as to its reality. Once acknowledged as such, it can make up for some defect or plug a hole, before – in the best of cases – being transformed so as to open up a path towards a repressed scenario.

In the transference/counter-transference situation, analysts too are sometimes beset by doubt, when patients call on them to bear witness to the truthfulness of what they say actually occurred in reality. That kind of doubt often indicates that the patient is functioning in a psychotic way. It is coupled with a crucial existential doubt, in which the reality of the external world and the existence of something that is not particularly obvious are called into question. At that point, the analyst, undermined as to his or her function as analyst/interpreter, becomes paralysed – the mind goes blank – if he or she tries to evade the insistence with which the patient poses the question. It then becomes essential to acknowledge the reality of certain facts, in order to attenuate the faltering of the ego that the patient is experiencing – an intolerable uncertainty, which in fact cannot be decided one way or the other, as to what is true and what is false, what is real and what is imaginary.

There are, however, many potential impasses. As Federn pointed out, the classic form of psychoanalysis might lead to these and possibly have a perverse effect: the discovery, for example, that some patients make about having been raped by a member of their family, an event that they say occurred when they were one year old and of which they demand confirmation. What they mean by that is that the analyst must acknowledge – and say so in so many words – that it really did happen, that it is not a fantasy. When these patients do not get the response that they want from the analyst – who is focusing on psychical reality – the only road open to them, now that they feel misunderstood, is to discredit the analyst and put an end to the treatment. In such a case, however, what these patients are also giving us to understand is that enacting that disruption echoes the one that they feel in their ego.

Apparently quite different is the surprising comment made by a young female patient. After telling me that she had been raped as she left a nightclub but that she had no real memory of what had happened, she added, somewhat paradoxically, "I would prefer it to be a delusion." She felt very doubtful about what had taken place; she said that if indeed she had in reality been raped, it would be disgusting because sex is something that is degrading and intolerable. Faced with the threat of an imminent psychical disintegration linked to a sexual experience, the patient felt that the delusional temptation was a way of resolving that issue.

Delusional thinking and the obsessive search for a reality event come strangely together as indicators of some breakdown in the mind when faced with the impossibility of processing what is at stake.

When their mind is not structured well enough, it can happen that patients do not wait for the moment of truth in order to put to the test, in their own way, some confrontation with external reality; they do this via a scenario that they themselves provoke, one that is therefore really experienced – and usually in a traumatic way. Could this be said to be an example of the phenomenon of repetition? What is at stake, it seems to me, is quite different. It carries with it a question that has remained hopelessly unanswered up to that point. What comes to mind are patients who self-harm or who over and over again have disastrous sexual experiences, as well as those for whom a traumatic reality, as we shall see later, is either denied or on the contrary present to such a massive extent that, with all of its excitation, it can never manage to be integrated and processed. Any disorder that affects one's anchoring in reality cannot but have an impact on one's sense of temporality.

Reality and temporality: two notions that would seem to join together yet which paradoxically are contradictory when the idea of "actuality" comes into the picture. The "actual" category is not "the present" – the latter has an element of duration and as such includes the past and the future. With the idea of "actual neuroses" in mind, we can see that "actual" refers to a kind of temporality that is cut off from the past, one that involves only the here-and-now moment. As an attribute, it no doubt contributed over the years to a possible confusion between what belongs to the present and what corresponds to a here-and-now "actual-ness" in the narrow sense of the term. It is necessary to go back to the idea of actuality and take it to its very limits, because it sheds a powerful light on the way in which psychotic patients function.

The word "actual", from an etymological point of view, comes from the Latin *actualis*, "pertaining to action", before it later came to mean "present" or "current". It is indeed active and effective as a defence. It has a hold over patients, forcing them constantly to make sure that they do in fact exist and, in the confusion and collusion of the categories of time, to verify, via a range of stratagems, the reality of each instant. Focusing solely on what presents itself, on what exists in the here-and-now moment, bears witness also to the transient nature of what is "actual" as well as to its effectiveness.

Used in its strongest sense, "actual" opens up a manner of functioning in which the past is not always absent, although the relationship between past and present is undermined. It is possible, with neurotic patients, to think about their refusal to accept the mourning process or a traumatic event in their past. The way in which they experience this kind of refusal and the consequences that it brings in its wake show that these phenomena are less influential in themselves than through the mechanisms that they bring into play: repression in neurosis, denial and splitting in psychosis and perhaps even a complete disruption. When Freud placed the threat of castration at the heart of his thinking, he was demonstrating the extent to which splitting linked to fetishism could be seen as a structured and organized form of defence. Splitting is a rejection accompanied by acceptation – doing things by half, thanks to which two contradictory attitudes coexist independently of each other: the acknowledgement of the absence of a penis and the denial of that absence (Freud, 1940a [1938], 1940b [1938]).

Psychotic patients, however, have to face rifts; with little confidence in their existence, they live in a state of emergency that drives them to enact, sometimes violently. They live in the immediacy of a world that is always slipping away, which they cannot catch hold of or which unravels – so that they have to grab it and rebuild it in their own way in order to fight the disorganization that threatens them. The "actual" is inextricably linked to "act" – which, too, is instantaneous and cannot be postponed.

In what Freud called the actual neuroses, the symptoms and other manifestations – most of the time somatic – do not possess the over-determined symbolic expressiveness of the neuroses. Similarly, the psychoses are not linked to infantile conflicts.

The loss of temporal boundaries brings several other phenomena in its wake: the ego may be paralysed and petrified, or it may expand and merge with the world, or it may even become fragmented. There are several possibilities, several ways of being, which correspond to the absence – or to an excess – of drive-related gratification, depending on the impact that this has on the ego. This is not so much a disturbance in the synthesizing function of the ego as, among other things, the impoverishment or the invasion of the ego.

Trauma and time abolished

"Actual" as a way of expressing a disturbance in time or as a solution to it sometimes becomes so far-reaching that it calls into question the very idea of continuity/discontinuity, as well as that of process. Paradoxically, although it is linked to speed, to urgency and to acting, "actual" in fact corresponds to a time of stasis in the gradual unfolding of mental life. Time is apprehended only from instant to instant, like an invention that has no premise, with no links to anything, no clashes, no beginning and no end. Perhaps it would be better to say that each instant is a beginning, a new departure, a new construction of life, something that has to be done over again and remade. Sometimes it is just the opposite – collusion and confusion of phases of time, when an undifferentiated past becomes mixed up with the present and attaches itself to it, with no interplay possible; any process that has to do with the relationship between the ego and other people or the world at large is interrupted.

Trauma has several meanings, given that it has gradually become looser and trivialized. To understand what failures in *après-coup* might mean for patients whose mental organization is psychotic, the definition that Freud gives in *Beyond the Pleasure Principle* (1920, p. 29) will be helpful: "We describe as 'traumatic' any excitations from outside which are powerful enough to break through the protective shield." In the ego's struggle on two fronts – internal and external – against too much sexual excitation (or if it is too powerful) such that the psychical apparatus fails to bind it all together, the importance of external reality is emphasized.

Freud's mention of the idea of something breaking through – evocative of a twofold impact, physical and mental – is a useful way of emphasizing the violence and the suddenness of this attack from outside (or at least experienced as such) and the horror that is felt when faced with an unexpected and dangerous situation, against which the ego cannot set up an appropriate defence system. Freud describes how fragile the consciousness system is when excitation from outside is so powerful that it puts the pleasure principle out of action and, having burst through the protective shield, breaks into the ego and overwhelms the entire psychical apparatus.

Trauma cannot be explained by the theory of deferred retroactive impact (*après-coup*); indeed, it is an obstacle to that effect. It prevents any access to it, either through colluding with it or as a result of the disruption that it entails. It gives precedence to "actual-ness" and prevents an initial repressed trauma, in which primal fantasies predominate (primal scene or seduction), from coming onto the stage and being played out again in this deferred and retroactive aspect which could make it meaningful (as happens in the case of the neuroses). It is as though instead of the second phase of the repressed traumatic scene, a real – or experienced as such – traumatic event breaks in and takes over, thereby defeating any *après-coup* process.

Adolescence, with the physical upheaval that puberty brings, can be either a flexible path from infantile to adult sexuality or a time of explosive crises that may lead to the psychotic temptation and to more or less pronounced and tenacious ways of functioning; this may go as far as disrupting or dissolving the ego's temporal frontiers linked to the Perception–Consciousness [Pcpt.-Cs.] system.

Bursting-in or breaking-apart – those are the available responses, depending on the specific circumstances: excitation getting out of hand, confusion and overflowing impossible to control, or perhaps an unravelling with its threat of emptiness and breakdown. It is to this kind of dramatic change that psychotic patients are subjected when the protective shield against excitation, with its links to the sense organs that Freud compared to antennae, cannot support for any length of time the perceptivo-sensory reality; at that point, paradoxically, an absence of sensations and an excess of them are often impossible to separate.

In Mr. X's case, the trauma gave rise to a disconnection from perception; the result was emptiness, with the threat that all mental activity might come to a halt. Ferenczi pointed out that "anxiety is fear of madness but transformed" (1955 [1994, p. 249]).

As a young child, Mr. X had been deported. After several years of face-to-face psychotherapy, he said: "For every child, trauma is a Holocaust." In his attempt to nullify the specific features of his own past history, he made a link between childhood, trauma and the Holocaust. The trauma of genocide and the trauma of childhood. Death and extermination at the beginning of life. The enigma of collusion between death and life.

In such circumstances, being able to formulate that particular joining-together and attempting to disentangle it represented a major step forward for Mr. X; he began to come out of the state of mental paralysis in which he had always lived. He had gone through life in an apparently normal way, but he admitted that he had never really lived – he had simply survived. He felt lost for quite some time, withdrawn, and with no signposts to help him on his way. Even nowadays it is difficult to reconstruct a chronology of parts of his past history. Generations appear to be indistinguishable at times. There is a great deal of confusion in what he says and he keeps repeating things in a kind of ritualized way. There are many recurrent themes that plug gaps – or, rather, are attempts at finding markers that he would like to have in order to be sure of some degree of continuity. There are no answers to the questions that haunt him and make him feel confused. He wonders about evil, about religion . . . In a kind of fragmentary and often contradictory way, he goes off into abstract thought and, faced with some enigma or other, lets it all drop.

For Mr. X, there was no connection at all between the existential difficulties that he encountered in his life and his childhood experience of the concentration camps – for a long time, indeed, he had no memory of that phase in his life, so that he began to wonder whether what he told other people as though it were a lesson that he had learned was really part of his own past history. He came to his sessions initially because his wife and his psychiatrist had told him that he had to talk about when he had been deported, but Mr. X himself did not think it either necessary or helpful, because he had no memory of any part of it. He began in fact to doubt whether he had indeed been through all that. It was as though time had come to a halt – or, better, what Ferenczi described in terms of "autotomy": in the animal world, the reflex that consists in tearing off parts of the body which are subjected to too strong an irritation or which are painful (Ferenczi, 1916).

Mr. X often had the idea that he should leave his wife and children, take early retirement and go into a retirement home – so as not to be a burden on them, not to harm them in any way. No doubt this would have been a repetition of being imprisoned in a concentration camp. It was also his way of denying the passing of time – or, rather, of breaking free of time, of a point in time when, in his view, violence and sexuality were mixed together and had to be rejected because of the danger that they represented. The opposite of a process of regression, this would amount to what Ferenczi called a "traumatic progression" (1949, p. 229); beyond sexuality and life, it provokes in the person who has recourse to it – and most of the time in spite of him- or herself – an excessive degree of maturity and vigilance.

Mr. X was cut off from his own past. He could re-appropriate it only with the help of outside elements that came from a collective memory, in the terms in which it was then expressed, brought into the face-to-face analysis. It was as though Mr. X needed the support of history to make contact with his own past and in so doing have the feeling that he did exist. As the treatment proceeded, he said that he wanted to contact some associations of former prisoners, to look for personal testimonies, become interested in them and feel more and more involved in the various commemorative ceremonies and manifestations.

He had clung for a considerable time to the here-and-now of "actuality", to that zone where time had no place, elusive. He said that "[his] body felt numb, with [his] arms swinging by [his] side, not knowing where to go, not understanding anything". That was a psychotic way of functioning: in denial, cut off from his body, from his past, with no possibility of regression . . . Mr. X would later be able to acknowledge that he had always felt himself to be on the edge of a precipice; he was then able to express his fear of breakdown and experience it at the same time.

In cases like this, when the analyst has no free associations to work on, he or she becomes, as Winnicott described, a kind of witness. It was necessary each time to confirm that the unthinkable event that was the Holocaust had indeed taken place and that Mr. X himself had been deported even though he remembered nothing of it, so that he would not find himself facing a wall of silence, emptiness or chaos. The analyst's role was to lend support to what Mr. X managed to say, vouch for the reality and authenticity of his past and of the traumatic event, calling upon the facts of history to do so, and attest to the traces of reality that until then, impossible to evoke, had been denied. It was necessary also to help Mr. X to construct, session after session, a form of continuity that helped him to break free of stasis, one that facilitated the emergence of temporality in which past and present would not be mutually exclusive or cancel each other out.

The difficulty in finding where to begin – an initial scene, as it were – was demonstrated through Mr. X's recent wish to make an album of photos. He did not know how to begin. Finally, he chose a photo that portrayed an empty window, with nobody to be seen. The ambiguity of photography – its function is to bear witness to the existence of people and places, but here it bore witness to absence and to a time that had gone.

The extreme situation that Mr. X had experienced gave him the impression that the world had gone mad; everything was "upside-down", as he put it, because, in the end, death awaits. For him, however, death and destruction had been at the very beginning of life. Zeitlin (Ertel, 1993, p. 109), one of the poets of that time of chaos and annihilation, says the same:

> How can I live? Your world has become a stain.
> How can I die? Death
> Is just a prologue to life.

Similarly, Paul Celan's (2001, p. 157) inverted psalm begins with a hymn of praise to God then becomes a message to No-one:

> No-one kneads us again out of earth and clay,
> No-one incants our dust.
> No-one.
> Blessed art thou, No-one.

Gradually, however, Mr. X began to have feelings that became more detailed as time went by. These were unpleasant at first – the smell of dogs' urine, the disgust linked to memories of latrines in the concentration camp, feeling that he wanted to vomit: the outside world, a physical world with its violence that had for so long been pushed to one side.

Mr. X needed some support from outside so as not to be annihilated, in a time that was before or even perhaps after all existence, a time with no temporality, on the edge of a precipice. It was only then that problems and issues relating to origins could at last be looked at more closely.

Confusion, time mixed up

This is often the case with patients whose past – from which they are completely cut off because it is too painful, too violent or produces too much excitation – does not really exist as a bedrock for their existence. They live in and for the present moment, in the immediacy of an "actuality" that is in itself uncertain and forever to be taken up afresh. Mr. A, however, was just the opposite – he was stuck, as it were, in a time in the past that was still part of the here-and-now of actuality, in a kind of hyper-reality.

At this point it would be helpful to keep in mind another of Magritte's paintings, entitled, somewhat strangely, *The Human Condition*, which dates from 1933. It is surprising in that it portrays something that runs counter to the human condition in terms of being part of a space-and-time that is in movement, with the capacity to think about oneself, from self to self, from self to other.

In a painting two years earlier, *Beautiful Captive*, Magritte had already made use of this disturbing questioning of representation. In that painting, the presence of another painting, standing on an easel in a field, emphasizes the impossibility of putting reality and a representation of it into perspective, with the necessary gap between them. The screen created by the painting within the painting, in a more obvious manner than in *The Human Condition*, does not so much reveal something that is hidden as fill up what is felt to be a gap in perception.

In *The Human Condition*, the painting on the easel is placed this time in the frame of a window. In making painting and landscape coincide as much as possible, it suppresses even more unmistakably the gap that any kind of representation requires.

Far from suggesting some kind of *mise en abyme*, with several surfaces or levels that would lend depth to it and evoke the idea of interiority, the frame of the painting is not separated from that of the window; similarly, art is no different from nature, it reproduces it in an identical manner such that there is a complete merging of the two.

Magritte's painting helps us to understand the relationship that some psychotic patients set up with the world. Time and space have no reflexive character, there is no depth; there is no longer any difference between frame and painting, between outside and inside. There is a kind of collusion between them, frozen in an exact copy, an equivalence, a merging one with the other, a complete absence of intervening space that would let us imagine just one different scene hidden by the painting placed in front of the landscape that unfolds on the other side of the window. The impossibility of any access to a multidimensional space-time is typical of the psychotic patient's malaise, with no markers because – at least in some cases – reality takes over everything. A degree of confusion that is close to a silent kind of madness, one that makes no noise.

Mr. A was being treated by means of psychodrama. After an analysis that had lasted some considerable time, he had gone back to his analyst to say to her, pointing to two chairs: "You see, we could put the child on this one and I would be next to him, to his left or to his right, and then each of us could at last say what he had to say differently." By that, the patient did not mean that, looking again at his past history, he was going to let the child buried deep inside him come to the surface – his intention was to separate completely from him, to unstick two people linked to each other over and beyond time, bound together, forever interdependent, with no distinction between child and adult, where time in itself was all intermingled.

The difference between this kind of situation and that of neurotic patients is no doubt the upheaval of what normally is (re-)constructed in what appears as the linearity of time – past, present and future are linked together by the power of desire, of memory and also of forgetfulness, in the continuity/discontinuity of mental life. The child in the adult that we are is the one we can imagine in whatever way we choose, depending on the ups and downs of our desires, of our memories and of our (re-)constructions – the child who lives inside us without invading us or living as a parasite. The child whom we call upon, in the course of our life, to satisfy our narcissistic and object-related needs, the child who inscribes us in a line of descent. It is only on that condition that our life can begin to unfold, in the necessary illusion of continuity, with a to-and-fro movement from adult to child, depending on the moment in time and on the different versions possible.

There are several kinds of non-temporality, depending on whether time itself is abolished, broken off or in complete confusion. In all cases, the loss of temporal limits goes hand in hand with various other phenomena, depending on whether the ego is paralysed, petrified, expanding, merging into the world or becoming fragmented. Each time, the past remains unintegrated, with no possibility of processing; there is no functioning of the perception-memory kind, with its before-and-after dimension. Sometimes there is silence or a fixedness that has no meaning in the patient's past; at others, there is a great deal of noise and agitation, with brutal and painful enactments. Whether it is a matter of something left unsaid and/or something experienced too vividly, the link with the infantile sexual past remains inaccessible as such. It is the principle of the absence of any historical perspective that characterizes the psychotic way of being, in which the past is there in the here-and-now moment of "actuality" or the here-and-now moment is divorced from the past. In both cases, there is no room for the present as such. With no past or a past that is all mixed up, the classic form of psychoanalytic treatment, the talking cure, is ineffective; no working-through of memories can be undertaken.

That is the paradox that some patients experience: the past is rejected as such but at the same time completely mixed up, so that mechanisms involved in remembering and forgetting, presence and absence, continuity and discontinuity do not function. The capacity that is required both for registering time and for erasing it is missing, hence the need for some other approach than that of the classic form of treatment.

Mr. A liked his first analyst but he did not feel understood by her. In the early months of his analysis, Mr. A had been seriously ill – he suffered from a somatic complaint for which he blamed his analyst, though he had never said anything to her about it. That accusation had remained buried deep down inside him – not denied but silenced – because, had he lost his analyst, that would have meant, in his view, that he would lose himself also. He acknowledged the fact that, during his analysis, he "had presented everything all neat and tidy" and was surprised to discover that in psychodrama "everything happened in a disorderly manner".

During the initial interview prior to setting up the psychodrama, Mr. A said: "Explaining myself, asserting myself means talking about outlines and shapes; from that point of view, I have the impression that I'm not properly enclosed. I really do have a problem with boundaries and frontiers. I always feel threatened both by what's outside and what's inside me. So I'm standing on a frontier, which is uncomfortable and impossible to hold on to because nothing is completely flat. Each time, there's always some kind of demand, from outside or inside, some tension, some moving around, a threat."

Those few sentences are an illustration not only of the way in which Mr. A spoke – in a manner that was simultaneously relevant and strange – but also of how he lived in the world; he was not inside a space of reality, of temporality, but "on a frontier".

When he was about eight years old, Mr. A had been abused both physically and sexually. What had not been a feature of his analysis – this is often the case – was that Mr. A was delusional in a kind of sotto voce way. He described this as "having a screw loose".[1] In the play scenario, it became obvious that there were moments of depersonalization, of dissociation, of inner silence and of his mind going blank, as well as times when he would have internal discussions, often with inanimate objects. In the course of the psychodrama, emerging from the mix-up of people, feelings and times, there appeared a mother figure who was depressed, full of hate, sadistic and mad; she, too, had experienced the violence of war.

In the "outside-of-time" that is a feature of classic psychoanalysis with a neurotic patient, what is said enables a to-and-fro movement between adult and child to be set up, with its meanderings and network of ramifications, thereby giving free rein to the possibility of interpreting. On the other hand, when no separation is possible, when there is no scansion, time becomes paralysed and weighed down, such that the unfolding of life and the expression of affects are hampered.

The reason for this is that "talking" is not "playing". Talking implies some degree of unfolding over time, words, thoughts and states of mind that succeed each other, even though their temporality may be shattered. To say how deeply one feels inhabited by a "despotic child", as Mr. A put it, is far removed from what takes place in psychodrama; here, the patient is very close to what he or she is experiencing. In Mr. A's case, for example, while the scenario was being played out, he had in front of him, present yet separate from him, the despotic child. It is even better when the patient can take on this role him- or herself. In the simultaneity or "dis-order" that reigned, given his surprise, there began to emerge emotions that were imprecise, violent or unable to be put in words and that until then had kept Mr. A paralysed in an indefinable and enigmatic zone. A "frontier" zone, without sexuality, in which past and present, beginning and end, birth and death became mixed up in a fixed state where confusion was always being renewed.

That is why in the present time of psychodrama, with its particular setting – I shall come back to this later – its many and varied scenarios, places, times and characters each physically present, it becomes possible to become unstuck from a traumatic past event; a dynamic movement can be set up, opening onto temporality in which past and present can be seen to be different. It becomes possible, too, to draw a distinction between the play scenario in which the characters are played by psychoanalysts, and the reality experienced in the one-to-one relationship with the play leader. Above all, thanks to the number of participants in the psychodrama and, therefore, to the fragmentation of the transference, splitting and projection can begin to evolve in the direction of a confrontation between opposites that until then were felt to be irreconcilable.

Mr. A understood that aspect very clearly. His comment was: "What I find interesting in psychodrama is that, to my mind, we work just as much on the 'how' as on the 'why'." He went on: "In my view, psychodrama implies several scenarios and playing them out – but that scares me because 'playing' implies flexibility, and flexibility is a threat . . . Yes, that's it, 'several' is the right word."

In one of the scenarios that he suggested, Mr. A was on holiday; he was cycling with two friends of his, a man and a woman. The latter two had normal-sized bicycles, while Mr. A, even though he was an adult, had a tiny one, a child's bicycle – "the little bicycle [he] had in [his] head," he commented. The entire play scenario had to do with the need to let go of his bicycle – and also with the risk that that entailed – so as to have one that suited him better. He spoke of his anxiety about emptiness, about voids; we told him that, as we moved forward, he would be the one who decided at what speed, at what rhythm.

The example of Mr. A shows how the role normally played by the protective shield against stimuli can sometimes be lacking. The attack against the frontier that separates inside from outside was so violent that he felt that he was wide open – wide open to confusion and to the overflowing that was at the same time difficult to give up because otherwise he would find himself on the edge of a precipice.

It then becomes important to re-assert the status of reality, intimately linked to that of temporality, either because the traumatic scene may still be present, hiding another one behind it, ready to repeat itself in the overall confusion and non-differentiation, or because, as a result of some disruption, it is completely wiped out, so that all that remains is mental paralysis or an invented delusion, given that the enigma of the foundational events remain unsolved.

Whether there is complete discontinuity, with no recognized past, or absolute and limitless continuity, with the mixing together of a past that is still in here-and-now actuality, the same massiveness and immediacy will prevail over any possibility of mental processing. In both cases, silence, with the avoidance of pain and of hate, and the tenacious persecution of an active and acting "actual-ness" lead the individual to becoming imprisoned in suspended time.

Amnesia and hyperamnesia both refer to a neurotic way of functioning. To use these terms in the case of psychotic patients means that we are moving away from an experience that is specific to psychosis – one that has to do with confusing or cutting off, with rifts, with confronting both a void and chaos. They also evoke the idea of memory or its absence, whereas here it is a matter of non-cathexis that goes all the way to not-registering and not-feeling because of the fear that feeling may prove too powerful. It is not a regression, which implies the re-emergence of earlier phases and patterns of functioning, linked to infantile sexuality and arising from memory and somatic traces; it is fear and the temptation of involution, of being drawn towards something that knows no limit.

PART TWO

A Space for Psychosis: From Writing to Psychoanalytic Psychodrama

4

Correspondence

The analytical situation aims to make what is said intelligible, so that the content becomes meaningful over and beyond the immediate sense of what is being talked about. That, however, is not its only role. Focused entirely on spoken language, psychoanalysis subjects both patient and analyst to the same verbal constraints. Whenever one or the other speaks or listens, the oral relationship, during the session, is also a sensory experience that some patients may find to be too intense, so that they become wary of it.

In control of the situation, the psychoanalyst enters "sonorously" into the patient's discourse. Initially, the analyst's voice, more than the words that are spoken, more than silence, will surprise, worry or reassure the patient. In the classic setting, the patient cannot see or touch the analyst, so that vocal and auditory exchanges – the only ones that are permitted – act as marker points. The patient is like a child who sings in the dark so as to overcome his or her fear – or, perhaps, it is the primary experience of separation from the mother figure that is being brought to the fore once again. Being left alone and coming together again are part of that strange experience that we call psychoanalysis, braced between a *hic et nunc* feeling and the intuition of something primary that, unable to be formulated, remains inaccessible – an unstable relationship that is disconcerting and disturbing for both of those involved. There is some degree of tension between what is being felt at a sensory level and the need to express things in words, with the sensory aspect participating both in what is said and in what is left unsaid in the relationship.

If analysis were to be stripped of its vocal aspect, of the melody of voices and the emotions linked to them, it would be no more than

"Words, words, words, as Prince Hamlet says" (Freud, 1926b, p. 187). Psychotic patients are just as distrustful of words as they are of relationships with other people – experienced as too close or too distant, and in both cases difficult to bear. They feel that words are too malleable and therefore dangerous. At times bereft of all meaning, at others too laden with meaning, words are traitors; they contradict one another and are painful. It can happen that the excess of the unformulated and the excess of what is expressed verbally lead some patients to trust only what can be written down. This is for them an extremely valuable substitute: a link is created by means of a concrete object that is visually reassuring because it can be controlled, and some distance can be maintained. Writing thus becomes a space that can be inhabited.

The unformulated, what can be formulated, and sensoriality

Freud had this to say about music:

> With music, I am almost incapable of obtaining any pleasure. Some rationalistic, or perhaps analytic, turn of mind in me rebels against being moved by a thing without knowing why I am thus affected and what it is that affects me.
>
> (1914a, p. 211)

Was that merely an admission, or was he in an exemplary and paradigmatic way describing what an analysis ought to be? Both patient and analyst must not let themselves "be caught up" and must hold in check their excitation and delighted pleasure by putting things into words, explaining them and looking for what caused such feelings – as though, in a somewhat simplistic way of putting it, things followed each other in a straight line that has to be looked at afresh: sensoriality leads to affect, affect to representation and oral representation to putting down on paper. From that point of view, the psychoanalytic relationship steers a middle course, where fusion and defusion take place at an appropriate distance from both extremes, from the two obstacles that have to be avoided, each at one end of the chain: on the one hand, the risk of being overwhelmed and getting stuck in sensoriality and, on the other, the infringement that writing denotes. How are we to break free of something that initially implied contiguity but is now wrongly seen as having to do with cause and effect?

From the melody hummed by the mother to her infant's babbling before the acquisition of language, from folk songs to an elaborate symphony, rhythm and tonality lie outside of words; they appeal to the sensory aspect that lies both below and beyond words, with echoes that are sometimes soothing and sometimes exciting.

The analogy with music may help us to think about what is usually understood in terms of a retrogressive – and therefore progressive – development. We have come to recognize that, in contemporary music, some sounds are aleatory and have nothing to do with being set down. Could this not be the case also in mental life, with its flaws and its leaps, its dysfunctioning and its failures, not forgetting its detours and its substitutions? With patients who are caught up in the psychotic temptation, we have to think again about our conception of time. There is a zone that lies outside of time, something that has escaped from time, in which issues involving beginnings are always coming to the fore. The creation of a scriptural space replaces that outside-of-time aspect.

From that point of view, the psychoanalytic situation is a dangerous one for psychotic patients, because the excess of sensations exacerbates the senses and gives rise to excitation and disorganization. Unable to be expressed in words, able to be expressed in words, expressed in words: it is in the gaps, in the silences that separate them, that writing comes on the scene, expressing and attempting to control what Baudelaire called "the ecstatics of spirit and senses" (Wagner, 1974). This is, in fact, a disturbance of the normal process of the perceptual system as described by Freud in "Negation": "The ego periodically sends out small amounts of cathexis into the perceptual system, by means of which it samples the external stimuli, and then after every such tentative advance it draws back again" (1925c, p. 238).

In counterpoint, all we need to do is mention the characters in Edgar Allan Poe's stories. They fascinated Baudelaire because of "all that imaginary world that floats around the nervous man and leads him to evil". In many of Poe's tales, characters suffer because their sensorium is so intense that they end up in a hallucinatory delusion and madness. In *The Fall of the House of Usher*, Roderick Usher suffers from a family illness the symptom of which is

> a morbid acuteness of the senses; the most insipid food was alone endurable; he could wear only garments of certain texture; the odours of all flowers were oppressive; his eyes were tortured by even a faint light; and there were but peculiar sounds, and these from stringed instruments, which did not inspire him with horror.
>
> (Poe 1839)

As the story unfolds, we see the explosive and disorganizing violence triggered by visions and noises when the distorted sensory elements – hurled forward, expelled and hallucinated – return in a reverse kind of causal and temporal logic that has something uncanny about it. External reality, cut off from any linking or continuity, is marked by terror and horror, until finally the House of Usher collapses and its owner disappears in the ensuing crash and chaos.

The sensorium has a twofold dimension. It takes in and emits, it organizes and disorganizes. For Freud, it is both soothing and capable of stimulating excitation. Bion emphasized not only the perceptual aspect of the sensory functions but also, and more importantly in the case of psychotic patients with hallucinations, their capacity to eject. He argued that verbs that have to do with sensations/feelings are in two directions – they both absorb and eject, which projective identification both reveals and thwarts. Seeing also implies ejecting via one's eyes. For Bion, as Rosenfeld also had argued, psychotic patients do need fragmentation – any unification of the object or of the self is felt to be threatening. Writing of a patient who spoke of the fusion and fission of objects in terms of nuclear explosions, Bion explained how that mechanism worked; he added, referring to projective identification:

> It can be stated in analytic terms as follows: He wishes to love. Feeling incapable of frustration he resorts to a murderous assault, or a token assault, as a method of disburdening his psyche of the unwanted emotions. The assault is but the outward expression of an explosive projective identification by virtue of which his murderous hatred, together with bits of his personality, is scattered far and wide into the real objects.
>
> (1967 [1984, p. 84])

Such indeed are the fears of explosion that we usually encounter. Patients who feel exposed to the violence of their drives when in contact with the object do need fragmentation. They sometimes seek out that intensity, in both pleasure and pain (agony), but more often than not they dread it and try to escape from it.

The echoes of the transference

On several occasions, Freud gave a great deal of thought to the capacity that psychotic patients have to set up a transference. He sometimes doubted that this could be possible, but at other times he did introduce the possibility, as he wrote in *An Autobiographical Study*: "Transference is not so completely absent but that it can be used to a certain extent" (1925b [1924], p. 60). He then went on to say something that is well worth studying in more detail: "But the chief consideration in this connection is that so many things that in the neuroses have to be laboriously fetched up from the depths are found in the psychoses on the surface, visible to every eye" (ibid.).

That somewhat ambiguous way of putting it does not explain what the phrase "so many things" actually covers; it could be understood as the absence of repression. I am tempted to emphasize that other phrase, "on the surface" – over and beyond what Freud is saying, this, in my view, corroborates the ideas of disruption and "actual" that I develop in this book as a basis for my argument. Connections have to be woven together and indeed woven afresh; but in patients who function in a psychotic manner, these do not fall within the province of the complex interplay of free association and the lifting of repression through interpretation. Patients who suffer from a disturbance of their temporality as a result of a distortion or rift in their ego that has upset, muddled or inhibited the unfolding of their infantile past have to be dealt with differently, in the here-and-now of the relationship.

Given their refusal or inability to set up connections with their past – too painful, too raw and too exciting, or, we could say, with an anterior/interior aspect in all of its depth – can we still talk in terms of transference in the traditional sense of the word, with its displacement of affects and imagos? Transference cathexis in psychotic patients is, it must be said, massive in nature, scorching and unstable. Far from being malleable and lending itself to the different rhythms and transformations of memory and of the work of the Preconscious in its articulation with the Unconscious, the psychotic transference does not stimulate all the modulations and resources that interpretation can bring. It is too impregnated with violence and excitation. It is experienced in the here-and-now of actuality and felt to be dangerous for both analyst and patient. What, then, can be transferred in the case of patients who have to deal with the denial of their past, given that their past is just too much for them?

Depending on the different forms of denial, disruption and rift and the various levels at which these come into play, there is a need for specific kinds of analytical setting and intermediary phenomena; these do not cancel out the transference, even though its existence in patients whose mode of functioning is psychotic has too often been denied. In itself liable to be disrupted at times, the transference gives rise to feelings of fear because of its overwhelming nature, the sheer power of its intensity. It is as though the analyst, focusing on his or her own associative thinking, found it impossible to take on board – or as though he or she felt too close to it, too fascinated by it, carried away by the dizziness of it all, with the idea that it might well prove dangerous, because the psychotic temptation is both frightening and fascinating. It clearly puts to the test the analyst's countertransference – the analyst cannot but be surprised by the inadequacy of his or her interpretative activity.

Following Rosenfeld, some have argued that the psychotic transference involves primary emotional experiences that are both powerful and undifferentiated. In this view, psychosis is rooted in a primary infantile dimension as a pathological form of an excess of projective identification that has to be interpreted.

The transference encounter takes place only when one of the two aspects of the transference can come to the fore – not the aspect that is based on repetition, but the one that has to do with the ego ideal being projected onto the analyst, thereby protected from hate, and with the wish to live, a wish that is still present in spite of the strength of the destructive impulses. The transference encounter is a response to the fluctuations of patients caught between their wish for complete freedom and their fear of fundamental solitude.

A new and hitherto unknown relationship has to be created and developed to the point where the presence of the object can be accepted and identification with the analyst becomes possible. For patients who live only in the avoidance of any time duration, in the immediacy of thoughts or feelings that are straightaway pushed aside or destroyed, the repeated encounters with their analyst in a clearly defined space are the crucial factor; these are shared inaugural moments, located in time, that constitute a beginning – and in these patients the very idea of origins and continuity is either denied or extremely problematic. The transference relationship that is to be constructed must of necessity focus on the present moment of the encounter.

What is transferred – that is, displaced inside the psychoanalytic situation – and therefore has to be encouraged to develop further, is the very difficulty that these patients encounter when they try to integrate a definite, stable space that includes temporality. The analyst – this is one of his or her roles – is then called upon to instigate and guarantee the patient's continuity. The analyst has to accept, for as long as may be necessary, the patient's denial of any past – or simply its absence – so that there can be set up a new experience that will be lived through by both participants as it unfolds, a shared history that is often elevated to the status of an ideal, in a timelessness that cannot accede to any disorganizing libidinal or aggressive impulses. This is what Evelyne Kestemberg (1978) called the fetishistic object relationship. The danger is that the wish for immediate satisfaction, born in the sudden emergence of an instant, might immediately be attacked and destroyed or experienced as too disorganizing. Thanks to the permanency of the analyst, these fleeting impulses may succeed in joining together, so that it will then be possible to move towards an acknowledgement of the transitory moment represented by present time, one that is different from the here-and-now of "actuality".

Thanks to that encounter, the presence of the analyst should enable some registering within a present time that until then had never been tried out, a bearable present that stretches to the point where it can at last fit in between a past and a future. This initial registering, in which presence and present come together, will be preserved; it is the opposite of a palimpsest that has to be deciphered – that of memory.

To accomplish this, the analyst's counter-transference is really put to the test, in a way that is quite unlike what takes place in classic psychoanalysis. It is not so much a question of associating freely, echoing what the patient may be feeling, being in close correspondence with him or her – all the while remaining strong in the face of threats of confusion or disorganization – and accepting the fact of being subjected to a particular tempo in which massive inhibition, violence and hyperexcitation alternate. It is more a matter of being present, without interpreting, and of accepting intermediate attempts at passing through chaos or emptiness. Writing letters to the analyst may be one of these intermediaries. For Mariani, writing letters in this way fulfilled that purpose. They accomplished the work of transition that was necessary before the object could be acknowledged as such and the "I", the first-person dimension, could at last come to the fore.

"I am writing to you . . ."

"For me," wrote Mariani in one of the many letters he sent to me, "writing is easy, even though there may be shortcomings. In addition, you're not sitting facing me. My tongue can loosen up more quickly."

In his sessions, Mariani hardly said a word. Indeed, he was in the habit of saying that he came not to talk to me but to see me. At the end of his sessions, he would leave, taking with him a picture of me that at times was so fleeting that he absolutely had to phone me between sessions to make sure that I was real and to put his mind at ease. My silent presence was all that he required, a presence that he wanted to be immobile and powerfully idealized. That was his way of holding on to me while keeping me at a distance. Another way of doing that was to send me letters.

Unlike the words that he transcribed in the correspondence relationship that he set up, spoken words seemed to him to be hollow or empty – although perhaps he would eliminate what he felt to be too full of meaning. What he had to do was to find or create a space between what could not be said in the excitation that he felt in our being together face-to-face and the emptiness that characterized the gap between sessions. In the sessions it was impossible for him to say anything that came from his own past because it was too painful; but by writing letters – indeed, thanks to that way of doing things – he was gradually able to set up a temporality, which, until then, had been denied.

In the overall unfolding of his psychotherapy, letter-writing started to become a regular feature when, as he began to integrate our relationship, Mariani gave up the idea of inscribing on his body, by self-mutilation, the suffering that until then had been impossible to express in words. As he did so, the voices that he heard and his delusional thinking began to fade away. He began to feel better but found it difficult to accept that – except through writing, in which both pleasure and pain could be expressed.

That was a turning point at the crossroads between repeating a past that he kept pushing away – unable to deal with it, he left it "pending"[1] – and the discovery of a new kind of relationship. It was also a new encounter in which, thanks to the fact that it was done in writing, Mariani could set up another kind of disruption, one that this time was paradoxically necessary so that he could go on with his psychoanalytic treatment and allow it to develop: it was a way of seeing me as different and separating him from his mother, a way of undermining the defensive system that had been in operation until then.

About his past, which was simultaneously too painful and too exciting, Mariani could say only a few things, a few brief items with no flexibility to them. The mere evocation of it was intolerable – his mother constantly ill had died young; he described her as a beautiful woman, courageous and loving. His father was said to be dangerous, with incest-related tendencies. As often happens with psychotic patients who have experienced breakdown and disruption, his past seemed only to have begun when disintegration set in – when he had his first phase of delusions. That episode seemed to have the hallmark of primary chaos.

The first few years of the treatment were difficult, with several delusional phases, suicide attempts and hospitalizations that disrupted our relationship. Mariani put me in an unchanging position whereby, as long as he kept on destroying himself, he would manage to spare me, so intense was his violence. Then, one day, after a session in which he had been querulous, he wrote his first letter to me. "I really must apologize. I am well aware of the fact that my aggressiveness is unwelcome, but it does represent the only and the ultimate means of defence that I have – and above all it is the only way that helps me put up with myself. But my role is not to be a torturer for you, nor are you to be the victim of circumstances for which you have no responsibility whatsoever."

The correspondence relationship that Mariani gradually set up had one particular aspect: it had nothing to do with reciprocity because, concerned as I was to maintain the psychoanalytic relationship, I did not answer his letters other than, in the subsequent sessions, tell him that I had received them and had read them carefully. That was a kind of acknowledgement of receipt, which meant that I was not deviating from my role as psychoanalyst, so that I could continue to set store by the sessions and the verbal relationship that was part of them. Those letters did, however, give some sense of continuity – an experience that Mariani had almost never known. Between sessions – in a second time-phase, as it were – he could go on thinking that I would not disappear and that he could create for himself, through addressing me, a space for existing.

The form that those letters took was relatively unchanging: always the same notepaper, the same format, the same length. A single page, the handwriting very regular and meticulously calligraphed, and always with one necessary marker – after the date, came the time of writing correct to the very minute, perhaps even to the very second. It was as though that bizarre element, repeated so many times, was the indication of the precise instant that, as it emerged, had broken the silence and done violence to absence. His first letter was the inaugural moment of his entry into a temporality that until then had been tightened up and compressed into the abolition of time.

The letters acted as intermediaries between two sessions so that in that interval, in that absence, neither he nor I would be destroyed or lost. They were receptacles for the violence that he felt towards me. The letters bore witness to his existence and to mine, like a breakthrough and an inscription in time that at last would leave a trace that could be located and marked, one that in its materiality would last. A present instant which, through the effect of anteriority, would become a past once it reached me – a letter destined to become the memory, or rather the imprint, of a moment in the past. The letters lent themselves to a confrontation between two temporalities, his and mine – and also between that of the sessions and that of deferred time. In the outside-of-time typical of the sessions, through the succession of times out of phase with each other, the movement from "actual" to present could be accomplished.

The transference encounter that then took place was like the assertion of a presence through which Mariani was able to acknowledge and accept what was always there, yet at the same time forever lost. An encounter made up of provocations and distancings through which, thanks to the correspondence between us, a specific manner of functioning was set up, one in which writing in its twofold work of filling-in was a necessary go-between: it both revealed and concealed.

"Words are ridiculous," said Mariani. He needed them to be like that so as to avoid being hurt by them, like those he had heard in his childhood – words that he had never forgotten. In fact, during the sessions, words filled gaps and blocked off more than they were used to make links and open things up. They hid more than they revealed and Mariani was aware of that. On the other hand, that first letter, in which he said that I was not to blame, was not a negation; it was the start of a link, one that inaugurated through writing – and, therefore, in his view something more lasting, more solid and more authentic – the possibility of a "correspondence" between us, in all of its polysemy. It introduced a new relationship in which the unfolding of passion – again, in every sense of the word: love and suffering – managed to keep at arms' length the hatred that it contained, so that only the pain was expressed.

"You seemed very distant this evening," he wrote, "and that really hurt me . . . I have such deep feelings for you, and you can hardly imagine the pain that I go through every day." Sentences like these, which one could almost think were borrowed from a seventeenth-century novel in the form of letters,[2] can be found in several of Mariani's letters. By opening up a space that was both scriptural and mental, they made encounters and separations easier for him to bear, so that he did not fall apart.

They were also a testimony to the difficulty he had in expressing himself during the time of the sessions, which he felt were too short-lived. Like the young poet of whom Freud wrote in "On Transience", Mariani demanded of things and of people that they be ideal and eternal.

> The idea that all this beauty was transient was giving these two sensitive minds a foretaste of mourning over its decease; and, since the mind instinctively recoils from anything that is painful, they felt their enjoyment of beauty interfered with by thoughts of its transience.
>
> (1916 [1915], p. 306)

The analytical situation that Mariani wanted to be "poetical" was based on the ideal and eternal beauty about which poets write and to which he aspired. Yet between ideal, ideally beautiful and transience, the writing of those letters made it possible to catch a glimpse of the other side – getting to grips with a different way of being in his relationship to other people. What was prevalent did of course have to do with a "fetishistic relationship" with the object, one in which I would be immobilized, just as he himself wanted to be immobilized – this was particularly the case in what he said in his letters, for example when he wrote that he came to his sessions only to see me, not to talk to me. The idealizing relationship made up for the emptiness and hopelessness that he felt when faced with an excitation that was too disorganizing. In the interval between sessions, the letters represented a movement towards a relationship of otherness. As he himself put it in one of them: "Letters have a soul, they are the shimmering of life."

It would, in this case, be a mistake to think that the treatment unfolded in a gradual, orderly way – or, for that matter, that it remained paralysed and dominated by ideal and idealized feelings. There were many upheavals, questionings, complaints and untimely enactments, so that somehow or other I had to keep us on course: the aim of all these provocations was to do violence to me and make me feel overwhelmed. Yet, as proof that he did acknowledge his analyst in all of her otherness, Mariani gave me some sheets of paper on which he had written, in the narrative present tense, some things that had occurred in his past. In that way, through writing it down, he managed to communicate a past that was still too vivid and share it with me. Writing opened up a space in something that was not condensed but all mixed up, confused. It provided a new foundation that supported Mariani in his endeavours to (re-)construct himself.

This brings to mind the transitional space, the "me/not-me" that Winnicott described. Mariani's letters, however, were more than that. They carried within them a reflexivity, a "between-me-and-me" aspect that is an integral part of acknowledging self and other.

Paul Eluard's lines (1926 [1966, p. 171]) come to mind here. Mariani had a particular fondness for that poet because poets find the words to express what otherwise cannot be said, the experience of opening up from self to self through the relationship with the other person:

> I separated from you
> But love still preceded me
> And when I stretched out my arms
> Pain made itself more bitterly felt
> The whole of the desert to drink
> So as to separate from myself.

Destined to be received and kept by another person, letters imply that separation and loss have become easier to accept. In that respect, they are signs of identity, experiences of transformation.

When Mariani sent me letters – and at one point their frequency increased – this was also a kind of violence directed at me as a person, a form of harassment. It was directly connected to what brought us together: the need to be able to express things in words. They obviously contained something personal, emotions and feelings that, according to Mariani, should not be expressed verbally. In that way, they brought about the beginnings of an "I" that could write, that could write to me and acknowledge its existence in different times and places and in different modalities. They participated in the construction or the advent of an ego that at first was locked into itself or completely disorganized; henceforth, it could make use of the first-person pronoun. In its very materiality, writing is a kind of creation, an act that constructs the existence of someone through the advent of acknowledgement of self and other, of narcissism and object relations, together with the connection that is an integral part of these relationships.

In his struggle against the wounds that life had inflicted upon him, against words that hurt, against insecurity, violence and destruction, Mariani – at last inserted in a temporality that was both retrogressive and pointing towards a future – wrote the following words: "I would like to be a little baby nestling inside your womb. That way I too could feel all your joy and all your sadness . . . You bring to reason the most beautiful of my better moments and my suffering."

It is quite possible, of course, to see in what Mariani wrote in that letter the workings of projective identification, in the sense that what is introjected in the analyst is what Mariani identified with after projecting it into me. But there is more to it than that. In Rosenfeld's view of that process, the wish to penetrate into the object highlights the question of temporality:

> The desire to enter into an object is not only determined by an omnipotent wish to eliminate the distance between subject and object, but also to get rid of "time". . . . The distance from the object or separation from the object is intimately linked with the awareness of the passing of time, because as soon as an object is desired, instant gratification of this wish is demanded.
>
> (1952, p. 461)

I would be more inclined to see a wish to identify with what the analyst was feeling, with the possible construction of a protected mental space – the image of the maternal womb in Mariani's letter – and the advent of a feeling of existence. This is similar to the two phases that Freud described in his study of the mystic writing-pad – I shall come back to this later – where there is both the presence of an available surface to welcome new inscriptions and a place where earlier ones are kept.

Mariani's letters helped to fulfil that role. They formed an inscription that could be preserved, both concretely and mentally. They represented what at last could be transcribed and transformed with respect to feelings, emotions and a past which, like the wax slab of the mystic writing-pad, could appear or not appear, but which in any case did not disappear.

But if Mariani were to be deprived of his better moments, would the risk then not be one of monotony and boredom? Although there may well be consequences in the future, his avoidance of two pitfalls seemed to grow firmer as time went by: on the one hand, melancholy – which made him lose himself in the kingdom of the shadows – and, on the other, that of the delusional temptation. Something that came from inside himself had henceforth been registered and could no longer be wiped out.

5

The materiality of writing

It has to be said that the origin of writing is a non-issue, because, given our present state of knowledge, we cannot come to any decision on that point. The question, nevertheless, does keep coming up, in an almost haunting manner. It is one way of expressing the ever-present question of beginnings, a topic that is forever being raised. The beginning of humankind, the beginning of the individual being, the beginning of writing – no answer can ever be satisfactory, except perhaps through the conclusion offered by transcendental thinking or in the incompleteness of a scientific approach.

Contrary to contemporary linguistic theories, writing had long been thought of as preceding oral language, because it was very difficult to give up the idea that there was something sacred about it. The status of a written text is indeed somewhat ambiguous: bearing the stamp of humankind, it is what makes meaningful the presence of human beings in the world, yet at the same time it goes far beyond them. Writing is related to something that is created. Myths and beliefs agree that it comes from the gods – an attractive hypothesis of primal unity that echoes another question, every bit as haunting: does writing have its source in the transcription of voices and gestures or, linked to the Creation, is it itself creation and presence?

Following Aristotle, for centuries the prevalent idea was that written words were symbolic representations of spoken words, so that there was a reduplication of what was heard – spoken sounds – through visual graphics. In 1891, however, Freud showed that there is a disconnection between verbal-auditory images and visual images. Words that are spoken are heard as coming one after the other, whereas when they are written down they can be seen all at once. Some forms of writing, however – Chinese, for example – do not go from thinking to feeling; they link them both together, condensing them into a single presence.

For some psychotic patients, in their nostalgia for primary unity, writing continues to have a sacred quality. They see it as giving access to an original language that was unique and universal, one that was offered to humankind before it was lost through being mixed up and multiplied. It resembled Schreber's "basic language" that he alone knew, elements of which he wanted to communicate through writing.

Generally speaking, what psychotic patients write has little to do with the pursuit of literary or aesthetic qualities. Their writings are characterized by urgency, by obviousness, by an appeal to sensitivity, and express the absolute necessity of survival that we sometimes find in art. Notes, narratives, poems – whether or not they are given to the analyst – have as their aim the creation of a space that goes beyond that of the analysis, reduplicates it, skirts round it and reinforces it.

A research study (Fonyi, 1994) was carried out on how 79 psychoanalysts belonging to various schools of thought reacted to their patients' writings. It showed that there were different ways in which these writings would be considered within the relationship based on "talking". Overall, however, the study confirmed the antinomy between writing and psychoanalytic treatment – proof that it was a form of resistance. The act of writing is seen above all as defensive and regressive, a way of evading something or a manifestation of the wish to be in control. The main reproach made by the analysts who participated in the study was that writing set up a lateral transference. For psychotic patients, however, the possibility of lateralizing a transference that is experienced as too overwhelming is a kind of intermediary, which, in this particular case, might be useful in setting up a relationship that is neither intrusive nor dangerous and in opening up a space to which until then they had no access. Some psychoanalysts did acknowledge, all the same, that by guaranteeing some continuity in the space-time created around the sessions, what patients wrote down facilitated the construction of that space-time, encouraged them to fantasize and compensated for their lack of dreams. Writing may also set up an appropriate distance whenever the relationship is experienced as being too close; somewhat paradoxically, it may guard against acting-out.

Through its materiality, through its concreteness, writing can provide a solid basis for the ego and make up for any threat of being wiped out and annihilated. How, then, should we describe that kind of writing? Micheline Enriquez has suggested the term "representative writing". Perhaps we should see in it a necessary artefact for constructing a sense of identity; in the following pages, I will use the term "liminal writing".

The body, the double-in-paper

In Plato's *Phaedrus*, Socrates narrates an old Egyptian tale in which Theuth, proud to have invented writing as a cure for forgetting and for ignorance, shows his invention to the god Thamus: "For this discovery of yours will create forgetfulness in the learners' souls, because they will not use their memories; they will trust to the external written characters and not remember of themselves."

The idea, then, is to encourage memories "of themselves". The "talking cure", set up on the basis of a theory of memory and of repression, is vindicated, inter alia, by the search for memories that are deeply buried, repressed. From this point of view, it is not difficult to see that, given its exteriority with respect to the analytical setting, writing can be an obstacle to the treatment – it could be seen as an enactment that hinders access to the patient's life-history.

Is it then a matter of retracing individual and group memories, as Freud saw it, to bring into the light of day and draw closer to something, which, like some vanished civilization, is revealed only piecemeal, little by little, with the aid of a few inscriptions and conscious traces?

The question, therefore, is how to enable some patients to have access to their memory – patients who, for various reasons, live with the loss of their past history, with its erasing or shattering, because it is felt to be too exciting or too painful. They are in an ahistorical state, as if memory traces were no longer able to be brought to mind or had perhaps never been registered. When these patients write things down, they are attempting to make sure that this new history, that of their psychoanalytic adventure, does not similarly go to waste; they want to know that the ego that is beginning to take shape can at last be connected to something palpable and concrete, even if it is only through that adventure.

For patients who are caught up in a psychotic way of functioning, the act of writing is a response to "actual-ness", to an "enactment" that is part of the relationship; instead of hindering it, writing becomes part of it and gives it some reality. By enacting what could not take place within the mind, writing – a material *corpus* that acts as an anchor – appears whenever any kind of identification or sense of identity proves impossible.

It is, therefore, ambiguous. When it is carried out, it enables us to grasp what is taking place in the analytical situation – what becomes of a sense of identity as it emerges through the struggle between life and nothingness in which the patient is engaged through a process of deconstruction/(re-)construction.

By this detour, which is also a means of recourse, the surprise of a presence that until then had remained formless comes to the fore; a new capacity is established, one that is open to reflexivity, and the patient can begin to possess a voice and body. A written inscription, emerging from the silence of thinking, can connect with new thoughts, because writing, as I have pointed out, is not simply a transcription or a reproduction of something that is said orally. Writing is an original production, a concrete inscription, a gesture that is physical, material and unifying.

Ethnologists say that at the heart of each of these activities, reading and writing, there lies the possibility of individual self-assertion to the same extent as the acknowledgement of the group norm that is part of them. In his introduction to a book that he edited, Daniel Fabre (1993), following the historian Michel de Certeau, emphasizes the non-passivity and intimate and specific appropriation that every reader brings to his or her "reading activity", despite the fact that the primary intention of teaching people to read is to domesticate and standardize all modes of thought. He goes on to study what he calls "everyday writings".

It is from a similar perspective – that is, that writing is the expression of a desire to assert one's singularity – that we should think of the "ordinary writings" of patients and of the point in the treatment when they appear as being the indication of a turning-point, of something that can be read and listened to: notes written on a piece of paper before or after a session, pages from a diary, autobiographical fragments, poems, letters, etc. These are all elements through which an "I" modestly tries to assert itself and commit itself. These revealing writings are crucial to the construction of the self.

For some patients who function in a psychotic manner, writing, unlike their body – long neglected – soon takes on the status of tangible reality. Here, we are far from Freud's approach to hysteria. Pointing out the inhibitions that those patients have with respect to writing, he insisted on the concrete elements necessary for it to materialize and on their symbolization through a representation of the sexual body.

> As soon as writing, which entails making a liquid flow out of a tube on to a piece of white paper, assumes the significance of copulation, or as soon as walking becomes a symbolic substitute for treading upon the body of mother earth, both writing and walking are stopped because they represent the performance of a forbidden sexual act. The ego renounces these functions, which are within its sphere, in order not to have to undertake fresh measures of repression – *in order to avoid a conflict with the id.*
>
> (1926a [1925], p. 90)

Conversely, the mechanisms of symbolization and repression that are at work in the neuroses show to what extent the manner in which psychotic patients function enables material elements as such to play an eminently structuring role. When the liquid that flows out of a tube and the piece of paper are not over-sexualized (i.e. seen to be dangerous because they generate too much excitation) but taken to be what they really are – concrete objects that can be used for support – they help the patient to construct a sense of identity that would otherwise be lacking and may even be used as a substitute for that sense of identity. When spatial and temporal representations are distorted, the relationship with writing in its material aspects can offer some kind of anchoring, in the sense in which Winnicott uses the term "indwelling"; for Winnicott, this corresponds, in the individual's development, to a phase in which the mind dwells in the body and where psychosomatic collusion takes place.

When dissociation or disruption threatens, the very presence of notebooks, sheets of paper, pens, pencils and ink carry the stamp of the person who is writing and end up becoming part of that person. This brings to mind Beckett's trilogy, *Malone Dies* (1958). As his life draws to a close, Malone-Macmann, who is dissociated, loses his notebook and his pencil. It becomes more and more difficult for him to find them again – they are the equivalent of his mental and physical reality, as his consciousness and his life are running out.

> With my distant hand I count the pages that remain. They will do. This exercise-book is my life, this child's exercise-book, it has taken me a long time to resign myself to that. And yet I shall not throw it away. For I want to put down in it, for the last time, those

> I have called to my help, but ill, so that they did not understand, so that they may cease with me. Now rest.
>
> (1958, p. 274)

One last presence, one final instant of creation, the last moment of control over other people and over the world, when writing and life coincide. This is the tragic side – that is, where the horror of the body and of its decomposing is uppermost – of what Laurence Sterne a century before had tried to describe in a derisively burlesque way in his book *The Life and Opinions of Tristram Shandy, Gentleman.* (I shall come back to this later.) In Beckett's trilogy, we do not see a metaphor unfolding; it is an enactment that comes very close to exhaustion and disorganization, one that can be expressed only through a form of writing that simultaneously echoes omnipotence and incompleteness, as Malone's last words make clear: "Never there he will never / never anything / there / any more." Unlike reading, for writing to leave a trace it makes active use of the body – the English word "handwriting" shows the link that exists between writing and the part of the body that is the hand. A partial body that is in action, on the way to the construction of a body image and its representation – unless, of course, it bears witness simultaneously to its inaccessibility and to its being sidelined.

Somewhat paradoxically, does poetic writing not take over from representation? Therein perhaps lie both the strength of poetry and the reason why it fascinates. For the patient Freud describes in *Totem and Taboo* (1912–1913, p. 56) as suffering from an obsessional neurosis, there is indeed a very poignant equivalence between her name as it is written down and her sense of identity. She "had adopted a rule against writing her own name, for fear that it might fall into the hands of someone who would then be in possession of a portion of her personality." Writing her name amounted exactly to her sense of identity; words in such cases have a magical power.

Writing, the double of oneself, another oneself that can be taken hold of, reminds us of the mystery of Man and the Creation, a mystery that is made of concrete reality and the vertigo of thinking. What actually takes place in the world may depend on thoughts and words linked to the animistic mode of thinking (Freud, 1933a [1932]). The fear of being dispossessed, of being faced with a void, led Freud's patient to give up her name in a magical act that was a preventive measure aimed at protecting herself; later, she gave up all attempt at writing, so that that too was cast out.

The reverse is also possible within the same kind of problem situation in an attempt to resolve the split in and impoverishment of the ego. In this case, writing, tied firmly to some kind of reality even if it is only that of the piece of paper, is used to fill in the absence of a psychical reality that has remained unformulated or has been erased.

Freud was very interested in the writings of ancient times – Hebrew and Chinese, for example. Leaving aside for the moment our way of thinking and our system of abstraction that bring together a concept and a word or a word and a thing, we must try to understand a different relationship with the "Real", one that is not representation. It is a way of creating or of re-creating through physical movement. In his book *Chinese Poetic Writing*, François Cheng (1996) explains the relationship between, on the one hand, writing and, on the other, calligraphy, painting, mythology and music.

> In the practice of this art, the calligrapher seeks to rediscover the rhythm of his deepest being, and to enter into communion with the elements . . . In the accomplishment of the unity of each character and in the balance among them, the calligrapher, even in the act of expressing things, achieves his own unity.

This implies that we have to think of language and reality as one and the same thing, not reified, but constantly evolving.

One of the examples described in Cheng's book is particularly apposite here: the experience of the poet who is describing a magnolia that is about to burst into flower. By looking so hard and long at the tree, he ends up becoming part of it. From the inside of the tree, he lives through an experience of blossoming. There is also the story of the painter who forgot the dragon's eye. To explain what had happened, he said: "If I had put in the eye, the dragon would immediately have flown off!" Poetry and painting, just like writing, are presences that come upon us, sensitive realities that are not subjected to the gap between signifier and signified.

Erasing the ego and writing

Private diaries are an important feature of adolescence, a period of transition that plays a pivotal role, the moment par excellence when writing goes from oneself to oneself at an age in which physical transformations to the body challenge and then strengthen one's gender identity. Supported by a feeling of something short-lived and by the wish to leave some trace that is a component part of the personality, writing would seem to be a kind of revealed-yet-hidden dimension that does not necessarily correspond to a sense of prohibition and transgression.

It is true that in adolescence these personal and secret writings, always felt as unsatisfactory by the young person who is putting the words down on paper – either as poetry or in a diary – and who will let them drop once the objective is reached, are probably always indicative of a quest for a sense of identity. In that activity, narcissism is very much a party to what is going on. The private diary is both a confidant and a mirror, a double-in-paper in which the narrator sees his or her own face and sketches an identity made of wishes, sensations and emotions that the words written down on it sometimes hide and sometimes reveal. For patients caught up in the psychotic temptation, writing – no doubt less rich and less diversified – is above all an action that aims to dig into and fill up the assertion that they exist.

What could the diary that Marguerite gave me to read have represented for her? I thought at first that it was simply an indication that she trusted me – a significant development in a relationship that until then had been extremely difficult, always having to be set up afresh.

This very emotionally unstable young woman – she had not gone very far in her studies at school, but did train as a florist – was always proud of the list that she loved to show people of the numerous jobs that she had had without ever being able to keep one for any length of time. With that same fickleness and lack of continuity, she "passed through" her sessions, as in her various jobs, without lingering; with the same disorderly restlessness that held her in its grip outside, she would narrate – almost in one breath – the chance meetings that she had, the changes in her workplace, the quarrels that took place and the various things that she did. Her whole life seemed to be made up of putting an end to things and breaking them off.

I was astonished to discover that her diary was made up of blank pages, except for a couple that were covered in clumsy and untidy writing, together with some loose sheets of paper on which were scribbled bits of sentences, scattered fragments of what could have looked like notes for an autobiography. The sheer blankness of the pages echoed Marguerite's incapacity to express differently in words the blankness, the futility and the emptiness of her being.

The lack of awareness of her own body and the absence of any sensations were illustrated by the ease with which she had sex with a whole series of partners, indistinguishable one from the other, and the very crude manner in which she told me about them. She had sex with anybody who asked her, but kept telling me that she was never satisfied, as though her non-cathected body was being used to continue the quest, until then in vain, for a sense of identity that seemed always to be out of reach. It was as though she would have a sense of existing only if she could manage to accept the idea of feeling something.

The fact that she gave me to read a diary that had so many blank pages was somewhat disconcerting, an avowal of the distress that she found herself in; it was another element in a relationship that was too strongly marked by destructiveness. That act was in fact the beginning of a relationship – immediately nullified – that contained its own revocation; closeness, like distance, was for Marguerite just as difficult to tolerate. Setting up a scriptural space, which in fact she did not give herself enough time to establish, would have been a positive attempt at recovery.

That situation made quite a contrast with that of Marie. After several years of face-to-face analysis, Marie offered me a gift: a completely new exercise-book with a beautiful hardback cover but with nothing written in it – what she wanted to do with it, however, was quite different. She wanted me to write a narrative of her sessions. This was the expression of her wish, at that particular moment in our work together when her delusion was beginning to fade away, that I keep her with me, inside me, that in a written document there would be the story that we were building up together over the years – a story the continuity and consistency of which she was beginning to feel. A desire to exist.

Absent as it were from herself, Marie had lived for a long time between dreams and reality, and at times she felt persecuted. She had never shown me the little notebooks in which she wrote down notes either before or after her sessions. She wrote down her dreams, her thoughts and whatever I said to her, the better to keep hold of me, as it were, and to keep hold of the experience that she had had during the session. In that way, having registered it in the material and concrete space of a sheet of paper, she might be able to construct herself in reality, over and beyond the time of the session, in the reality of writing. From time to time, she would re-read what she had written, as though to reassure herself, through making contact again with the intensity of what she had experienced, that both she and I continued to exist. Indeed, those notebooks, which she always carried with her in a kind of extension of herself or another herself, helped her not so much to remember as to construct herself, to become part of a temporality via the two spaces that were represented – that of the sessions and that of her writing up her notes. The blank pages of the notebook that she offered me were indicative not so much of a lack of a solid foundation as of a possibility of projecting into the future. She put her trust in writing and only in writing. She felt that spoken language could be trite, diverted, manipulated. It enables you to say one thing and the opposite. She could keep control over the many possible meanings only by remaining silent in her everyday life. Writing alone, because of its fixed and unchanging character, could give her some guarantee of the reality of what she was experiencing and reassure her. In her view, writing could not lie. The permanency of writing implied that of her own existence. For Marie, the act of writing and what was written down had a kind of sacred character.

The relationship that she set up was for a long time characterized by confusion, incoherence and blurring because it was quickly caught up in sexual excitation; giving me that notebook was a turning point. Her relationship to her body, over and beyond excitation, confronted her with loss of identity and emptiness. She masturbated compulsively (and was ashamed of doing so), suffered from time to time from anorexia, had had abortions – all of these were a matter of filling up and emptying her body experienced alternately as elusive and as self-destructive. After many vagaries, Marie succeeded in setting up a more coherent relationship and in becoming more aware of herself. Her ego began to be constructed. The outline of a narrative began. Memories emerged and took shape. Characters other than pale evanescent silhouettes, eminently interchangeable, began to take on a more definite aspect. During all these developments, writing was there to act as a relay or as a marker.

In a society in which, from infancy on, writing is omnipresent, it is not surprising to discover that it may be of comfort to some people. Writing has a double aspect: it sets the imagination free, but it also directs, orientates, organizes and demands that everyone receives and integrates its watchwords. It may even act as a substitute for deficiencies in thinking. When some patients feel too powerfully confronted by the demands of everyday life, in their moments of dispersal, fragmentation and fear of emptiness, it is through writing and its materiality that they can find a way to navigate through their phases of derealization.

This was the case with d'Orlando. His impression that he was disappearing was so powerful that he could not face up to the gap between two sessions without some damage occurring, without his feeling that we might both of us be destroyed or otherwise disappear. He began to draw up lists of the people whom he was due to meet and to programme what he ought to say or do, how he should behave. These were not simply aides-memoire or "reminders", the kind of thing to which many people have recourse. Writing things down prevented him from disappearing or being lost in a confused state that would quickly engulf him. He had to be able to keep hold of what otherwise, in his relationship with another person, would become empty, to hang on to what he himself was ejecting.

A brilliant student, when he felt that he had no "mental locus" for himself, the best he could do was to live inside books. He would always carry some around with him, in big bags that he would put on the floor near his feet during his sessions. He would feed on them and spread himself out inside them until it came to a point where they would be unable to contain him. He would then no longer be able to do any work. Confusion and excitation seized hold of him. The delusional temptation was not far off. Fortunately, a minimal kind of writing, no matter how insignificant, would then take over and enable him to set up at least a few boundaries.

When he was an adolescent, he and his sister, to whom he was very close, were separated. That plunged him into a feeling of ineradicable solitude; the emptiness that kept its grip on him had at one point pushed him into attempting suicide. When an increase in excitation got to the point that it overwhelmed him in an intolerable way, making him lose his bearings, writing sorted the situation out. The lists of things to do and behaviour to adopt, once they lost their automatic reflex quality, helped d'Orlando to re-invent himself at any point in time. They reassured him that nothing more would be lost and that he would not lose himself.

Sarah, too, had recourse to a similar ruse when, for the first time, she had to reply to an offer of work that she felt would be invasive and threatened to disorganize her. Sarah, who was in her thirties, still lived with her parents and did not feel that she needed to go out to work; she was completely taken over by her mother's experience of having been deported. She kept putting off the time when she would have to leave home, losing herself for many years in writing out job application letters and trying to stop the passing of time.

When she was about to start her first job, she spent the previous day writing out in detail all the movements and gestures that she would have to make. From the very beginning, her relationship with her body – which she fed less and less – began to change; she became so thin that the whole situation began to look worrying. In her struggle against herself, I could see that, physically, she was melting away and disappearing. As though there were no longer any match between Sarah herself and her body, she needed the presence of paper as a relay. On the way to work, she read and re-read her notes, not so much to keep them in memory as because she had to be sure that she could take support from these indicators of her existence. Paper, a more reassuring substitute because it was tangible, was like a small part of reality, a space that was completely delimited, mapped out, so that, by clinging to it, she could be sure that she would not lose herself.

In such cases, the work of the mind and the professional work that is part of the outside world come up against the same difficulties. Etymologically speaking, the word "*travail*" ("work", in French) has to do with a form of torture.[1] In neurosis, work done on the libido leads to the lifting of inhibitions related to the workplace. Psychotic patients see work as totalitarian, representing not so much a step forward on the path to recovery as a confrontation with the unbearable command: "In the sweat of thy face shalt thou eat bread" (Genesis 3, 19). Suffering and destitution, as after the revelation of sexuality and the Fall. For someone who knows them well enough already, they have to be avoided – denied – at all costs. The refuge is the false paradise of early infancy, and perhaps even of non-existence. Going all the way back to a time before birth, to Limbo, the liminal *locus* of an eternal waiting.

Sarah's attempts to be in control bear witness to the extent to which her fear of breakdown and annihilation had to do with an experience of primitive agony, as though her mother, who had gone through so much, had not been able to give her a time of non-existence, which is a necessity for existence itself. How can the connection between one time phase and another be re-established in people for whom every single moment is a threat? For Sarah, psychoanalytic psychodrama, while her analysis was still ongoing, helped her to move from one to the other.

"Representative" writing

Micheline Enriquez's (1978) paper on representative writing illustrates and corroborates the relationship between a certain kind of minimal writing and the need for a solid identificatory foundation. The clinical cases that she reports, more extreme than those I have described here, are well worth mentioning. They highlight, interpreted perhaps in a slightly different way, the recourse to operational enactments that, in particularly crucial moments, have as their aim to delineate and redefine space and the body.

Is this a purely instrumental action of reassurance or an act of creation, of re-creation? A desperate attempt to ensure, through naming and tracing, that the death drive cannot win? Recourse or return? Those are the questions.

In her description of Fanchon, Micheline Enriquez says that, for the patient's adoptive mother, her body was simply "an inhabited bodily machine". That case has many points in common with what I have described as a quest for a sense of identity through writing, but in a more systematic way. To fight against the temptation of suicide, the patient wrote short sentences on little bits of paper that helped her to plan out her day (toilet, weigh myself, eat, get washed . . .). These fixed elements were a regular occurrence; more mobile written sentences were attached to them: "Don't leave anything behind, don't leave any traces, check things as you go along." "It is those phrases," said the patient, "that give me my true identity, much more than my other identity papers do." Far from any possible interpretation as to content, as Enriquez points out, this is more like an attempt at pulling herself out of nothingness so that her self can emerge.

Similarly with the other patient whom she describes. During an anxiety attack while he was travelling through a country area in France, the patient completely lost his bearings and had to get up in the middle of the night and write: "I am in a hotel bedroom, in the Hotel Terminus, 10 avenue de la Gare . . . The wallpaper is such-and-such a colour . . . I am going to look out of the window, I can see the railway station." Writing is used here as a concrete memory trace of what appeared to be doomed to destruction. Micheline Enriquez says that naming things through writing enables the physical element and "the world element" to be recovered.

In both cases, there was no internal perception of the person's body; that perception was becoming undone internally. The lack of such a perception meant that writing and the physical movements that writing demands became a substitute for the body. The second patient said: "It's as though writing helped me to get a skin back"; that patient, suddenly emptied of what was inside, was searching for an overall shape, an envelope or a (re)creation of himself.

I completely agree with Micheline Enriquez's description, in which we see the "actual" quality of an act that appears as a bastion against anxiety about death, destruction and dissolving; this is linked to hate that has not been properly worked through. She is correct, too, when she points out the possible function or rather functions of this kind of behaviour, which occurs at moments in time when the individual seems to be fading away and disorganization and chaos reign – an attempt to sort things out, to reorganize actions and gestures, to redraw an external world that has lost all meaning and all reality: "Through the hand movements that [writing] entails, the patient makes a personal mark, sorts out his sensory impressions, appropriates them in a time and *locus* that are closely defined." She emphasizes also the need for the body to be brought together and reunified through setting up a tangible form of reality in which what is perceived is registered.

Micheline Enriquez notes that this kind of writing is "formal", in that it "lays greater weight on form than on meaning". The name that she gives it is "writing, the vocation of which is representative or figurative". "This type of locating, in spite of its fragile character, enables access to a representation of the self, without any mirror or word spoken, one that is based only on cathexis of the sensorimotor activity."

What, however, she does not in my view highlight sufficiently is the extent to which these patients are cut off from their past, such that any kind of regression process is impossible. At what level can they place themselves when memory is blocked off? Is it not at that point a new and even original experience? That question is important, because it has also to do with certain technical aspects.

Is it possible to move towards a "primary" text made up of bodily memory traces without going through regression – something which these patients resist as much as they can? Is there not a contradiction, or at least some ambiguity, when Micheline Enriquez, in her "concluding hypotheses", argues that this kind of writing has to do with figurability – a basic condition for something to be represented, as in the case of dreams – and with primary processes, hence the designation "representative writing"?

Her second patient, who went through an experience of derealization in his hotel room, also wrote a poem about the railway station, an initial piece of writing that was "representative" in that it created, she says, "a potential space in which were fulfilled the necessary conditions for the emergence of a fantasy activity expressed in this case through the medium of poetic writing".

Is there such a great difference between these two forms of writing? Without making any value judgements, we could imagine that for the patient concerned his initial writing and his poetic writing were closely connected; his experience, unlike that of the dreamer, was not based on primary processes that opened onto the possibility of putting words on what was happening and making it meaningful, through interpretation, thus enabling processing to take place. In general terms, is poetic writing not also a sudden emergence of something? In both forms of writing there would seem to be a similar attempt at presence, the same traces of reality taken up on the spot through words – in words, we could say – when perception and designation come apart.

Calling this kind of writing "representative", together with the idea of "figurative", would seem to indicate that a primary text exists somewhere and must be recovered, thus creating some degree of confusion.

If we see things more in the way that Lyotard, following Merleau-Ponty (1961 [1964]), calls not figurative but "figural" – the emergence of sensitivity – this kind of writing helps us to understand the psychotic way of being. While preserving the enigma of the perceptual, it undermines somewhat the distinction between experience and essence, imaginary and real, visible and invisible. In the "figural", what is invisible is not set apart from the world of sensitivity. It is expressed in a contingent manner, next to what is visible, without any distinction between the two. Like poets, in that special time that presides over poetic creation, psychotic patients are standing on the threshold or in the margin of a symbolizing mental activity.

It would therefore perhaps be better, as I shall explain in the following pages, to speak of "liminal" writing – this would require us to look again at how things are registered and at the relationship that Freud described between words and things.

6

Imprinting and the effects of reality

The road that Freud followed, from the "Project" to "A Note upon the 'Mystic Writing-Pad' " (1925a [1924]), took him from a neurophysiological standpoint to a metaphorical representation of the apparatus of the mind. One result was that the idea of registering something in memory – and therefore that of written signs and mental writing – gradually took on a more differentiated meaning.

The letter that he wrote to Fliess on 6 December 1896 marked a turning point in what Freud called "a new psychology". "Thus what is essentially new about my theory is the thesis that memory is present not once but several times over, that it is laid down in various species of indications" (1950 [1895], p. 233).

The "Project" began with a description of transmission by neurons, and it was on that basis that, in the letter quoted, Freud began to draw the picture of the mind that would later appear in chapter 7 of *The Interpretation of Dreams.* The process of memory, with its various recordings and surfacings, gives a more detailed description of how things are registered in the Unconscious and Preconscious and makes clear the actual nature of memory. Freud then left to one side the idea of something being written in memory and focused more on describing the psychical apparatus in terms of more mechanical metaphors – microscope, telescope, camera. The mind was thus seen as an instrument in the service of psychical productions. The systems, with their functions and processes, which make up the mind confirmed the intuition that Freud expressed in that letter to Fliess: a domain in which, over and beyond its neurological aspects, the psychological element has a role to play.

The unconscious is the second locus of transcription, after that of perception. Out of the unconscious only memory traces can emerge.

These are inaccessible to consciousness, which does not preserve them "for *consciousness and memory are mutually exclusive*" (1950 [1895], p. 234 – italics in the original). It is only thanks to a third form of registration linked to verbal representations – that of the preconscious – that access to consciousness becomes possible.

At the very heart of Freud's thinking was the question of how memories, in the metaphorical form of a written text, could be preserved or erased. Memory – and forgetting, which is necessarily linked to it – is tolerated only through the presence of another and identical writing that is momentarily erased yet still accessible: that is how the apparatus of memory works – nothing of what has been recorded is ever lost. That is also how the perceptual apparatus functions.

In his encyclopaedia article on "Psycho-Analysis", Freud says that the patient is not invited to remember things but is "required to put himself in the position of an attentive and dispassionate self-observer, merely to read off all the time the surface of his consciousness" (1923 [1922], p. 238). When the relationship between psychoanalyst and patient is seen as communicating from unconscious to unconscious, this modifies the very idea of memory and gradually gives to writing, to a written text, a different status – that of a text that has to be translated.

The patient, then, makes use of free association to read what is on "the surface of his consciousness", while the analyst has to catch hold of the patient's unconscious by means of his or her own unconscious in a state of evenly-suspended attention. These are the complex operations that are necessary for deciphering a text that is both present and absent, forever slipping away, once the idea of recovering the supposedly original version is abandoned.

"Registering" and "transcribing" – the only way in which Freud could describe, not the mind as such, but the fiction of the psychical apparatus and its workings – are both fundamentally metaphorical. As their meaning shifts, they gradually take us further away from the neurological approach so characteristic of the "Project".

Registering, transcribing, translating – these metaphors that haunted Freud all have to do with a text being written down. In spite of the ongoing temptation to give some kind of concrete and scientific reality to the psychical apparatus, the movement towards a metaphorical conception became more and more pronounced; it is in Freud's paper on the "Mystic Writing-Pad" (1925a [1924]) that it really comes into its own.

In that paper, Freud again takes up the idea of the registration of real "psychical writing" and manages to find an answer to the question concerning the difficulty involved in reconciling the preservation of what is registered and the presence of a receptive surface that is blank and always available. The mental apparatus, with its different phases and movements, is similar to the mystic writing-pad but not identical to it; for the mind, it is not a matter of materializing something that remains fixed, unchangeable and limited.

Freud's analogical way of thinking is here developed to its utmost. He does not let himself be imprisoned in what could turn out to be simply a comparison; having opened up the pathway, he succeeds in reaching a new stage in his thinking – that of a reflection on temporality.

Discontinuity as a way in which the mind functions is what connects us with time and enables us to perceive it, even though we have to re-establish, in ourselves and with some types of patient, the continuity that presides over our life with its starting point, presumed or reconstructed.

The idea of reading off "the surface of consciousness" (Freud, 1923 [1922], p. 238) and "reading a lengthy book of pictures" (Freud, 1895 [1893–1895], p. 153), if we think about the metaphor, takes us away from the somewhat simplistic notion of recovering a primary experience that would amount to no more than reading and re-writing a text that has already been experienced and written down – a biography of the patient, with its different episodes and events, in a linear unfolding that we simply have to find again, whereas in fact it has to be (re-)constructed. It is at this point that the movement towards a mental form of writing, in all of its depth and different versions, comes to the fore.

We have to think about how certain patients function in this respect – those in whom there are deficiencies in their internal system of registration or interruptions between different phases of registration. These flaws give rise to disturbances in temporality, such that remembering can hardly be made use of at all.

These patients resort to enacting what cannot be part of the continuity/discontinuity of mental life. Whenever any kind of identification and sense of self becomes too difficult, they get lost in the absence of limits so characteristic of origins. Writing, a material corpus to which they can cling, offers them, among other things, a space in the mind that does have boundaries. Similarly, psychoanalytic psychodrama, through the complex modus operandi that it represents, provides them with a suitable mental framework.

Mental writing

The example of the mystic writing-pad helps us to look more closely at how the perceptual and memory systems function and to understand them better. They function on several levels, including those involved in the reception and preservation of perceptions, and offer some answers to the questions of memory, forgetting and repression that are a constant feature of Freud's writings.

That model, all the same, does not correspond very well to the way in which psychotic patients function. It does, nonetheless, given its focus on the internal and external perceptual systems as sources of excitation, emphasize the impact of external reality and what occurs whenever this proves overwhelming.

It also makes for some comparison with another approach, that of individual psychoanalytic psychodrama, which involves both physical and psychical reality. That technique offers patients who function in a psychotic manner a better way of registering reality and, in so doing, gives them the opportunity to re-appropriate their self and their past.

The mystic writing-pad helped Freud to see how the need to preserve memory traces could be reconciled with making room for new registrations. The pad is made up of a piece of translucent waxed paper over which is laid a transparent celluloid sheet; this is then placed on a slab of resin or wax. Writing is done with a stylus on the waxed paper, so that it can be seen when in contact with the slab; in the absence of any contact with the slab, no writing can be seen, but it remains etched in the wax.

Unlike a sheet of paper on which a limited number of fixed inscriptions can be made or a slate that has to be wiped clean before anything new can be written on it (here there is no limit to the amount of possible inscriptions), the mystic writing-pad, just like the perceptual apparatus, enables an alternation between inscribing and temporarily rubbing out, between remembering and forgetting or repressing. Writing may well be the guardian of memory, but registering something in the mind does not give rise – unlike the mystic writing-pad – to an inscription that remains unaltered.

> If we imagine one hand writing upon the surface of the Mystic Writing-Pad while another periodically raises its covering-sheet from the wax slab, we shall have a concrete representation of the way in which I tried to picture the functioning of the perceptual apparatus of our mind.
>
> (1925a [1924], p. 232)

This kind of functioning, however, as I have pointed out, does not correspond to the psychotic way of being, with its all-or-nothing constraint. When the perceptual element becomes overwhelming, disruptions occur, with perceptions being either rubbed out or not registered.

In his comparison with the slate, Freud does mention one danger but without going into more detail about it: that of an inscription that may be rubbed out and therefore disappear. Another danger in some cases is that of absence of or deficiencies in the protective-shield function of perception. Hence the usefulness of a "protective sheath . . . to keep off injurious effects from without" (1925a [1924], p. 230).

If drive impulses do generate failures in the internal system of registration or deficiencies in the protective-shield function of perception, the necessary interplay between continuity and discontinuity can no longer work. With reference to the temporal dimension, Freud concludes his paper on the mystic writing-pad with the comment: "I further had a suspicion that this discontinuous method of functioning of the system *Pcpt.-Cs.* lies at the bottom of the origin of the concept of time" (1925a [1924], p. 231).

Time and perception. Continuity and discontinuity. The metaphor of the mystic writing-pad helps us to understand, *a contrario* perhaps, psychotic functioning, in which continuity and discontinuity do not possess the alternation that is necessary for the acquisition of temporality.

Saturation and/or evacuation make any coherent temporal representation impossible such that no progressive or retrogressive processes can be set up. Patients who suffer from disturbances in temporality have to find a way, thanks to appropriate treatment, of moving from here-and-now actual-ness to the dimension of present time.

The case of Mr. Zapper

"I find it very difficult to say anything during my sessions . . . I have the impression that I don't have a memory, I seem to zap very very quickly whatever happens to me, so that I can't give very much to my psychoanalyst . . . things to think about or work on."

Mr. Z said to his analyst, who referred him for psychodrama while continuing to work with him in psychotherapy, that he could not give her anything, because he was unable to look inside himself in an attempt to process his past experiences. He made it impossible, too, for the analyst to think, because his main way of functioning was by means of dispersion, disappearance and wiping out. It was as though no new inscriptions could be made – and no previous ones could be brought back as memories. Evacuation was constantly being enacted. The lack of memory and its corollaries – confusion, dispersion, emptiness – were, all the same, indicative of the threatening presence of something about to overflow and to overwhelm him. In circumstances like those, how could he ever manage to take in the complexity of relating to other people or cathect representations?

It is no easy matter to draw up an account of the various scenarios that were played out with Mr. Z in his psychodrama sessions. None of the classic elements of psychodrama – playing out fantasies, conflicts, defence mechanisms – based on drive impulses and the possibility of representing them were a feature of his treatment.

Mr. Z could never remember anything, suggest anything or make any comment. When, during the initial interview, he was asked if he had dreams, he replied: "I don't remember my dreams. It's the same thing, I think I must zap all that, evacuate it, I don't really remember. Sometimes I get feelings that might be pleasant or unpleasant, but I don't remember anything about them." He went on to say, referring to the projective tests that he had been invited to take, that he had felt unable to invent any stories. He was able to describe what he saw, but he could not imagine anything. He added: "In all seriousness, I don't know whether I can actually think, no, no. I think of things in general, about life in general, even though I know nothing about the how and why of all that. There are some big existential questions still around, and I often have adolescent-type concerns like – what's life all about?"

Mr. Z seemed therefore to have no memory, no imagination; it was as though he had no connection with reality or with time. It was always very difficult to choose a play scenario. Most of the time, although he was part of the play even if he did not really play out anything directly, he listened to what was being said and watched what the others were doing. Some typical situations were taken up several times and repeated: patients in the waiting room, people he had met in a café, actors in a theatre company. Each of the characters, suggested by the play-leader more or less with Mr. Z's help and played by the therapists, were an attempt at expressing his malaise, his wish to be free of all his problems, his distress, his violence, the terrible loneliness that he felt. In their play, the therapists were very attentive, gave a great deal of themselves, said many things and often suggested various kinds of hypothesis, creating, from what they themselves could feel, characters who expressed their malaise, their violence or their understanding of how painful distress could be. There was nothing that could be seen as an evocation or repetition of some past event in all of its possible versions. It was necessary to start off from the nothingness that Mr. Z was experiencing, the emptiness that both worried and protected him, was part of him and destroyed him.

We spent a long time with him in what was a kind of wilderness or descent into hell; he could express his pain and his hate only through alcohol or drugs or by de-cathecting everything to the point of wanting to kill himself – so that we had to keep a tight hold on what we played out in the sessions.

It was when one of his children, a boy, was born that Mr. Z became severely depressed – much more severely, he said, than anything he had known until then. He had a breakdown that required hospital treatment for a month. In the first week following the birth of the baby, he was in the grip of such severe anxiety that he was unable to get any sleep. He said: "The baby, at first . . . he cries. When he cries, there's a reason for it . . . either he's hungry or he's having a nightmare." That would seem to indicate the existence of primitive agonies.

Of his own parents, Mr. Z said very little, except for the fact that they were never very "present" in his life. He had nothing to say about his childhood – not even a word about the emotional hunger or the terrors that we assumed he must have experienced. While one scenario was being played out, we learned – incidentally, as it were – that, when he was a young adolescent, a close relative of his had seduced him. With that young woman, he had sex very early on in life; he said that it was "quite complicated", then went on: "It was very nice, I felt loved, pampered, there was somebody to take good care of me. It was nice, yes, it was." He said that that woman had given him some kind of existence – but that she had both loved and destroyed him.

There were scenarios in which, through classified adverts in newspapers, he wanted to meet people who, like him, intended to commit suicide; there were others in which his wish to be helped was expressed in family get-togethers.

The day when, in tears, he said that his psychoanalyst was the only person who understood the emptiness that was and had always been in him, that he wanted somebody to take him into his or her arms, that he wanted to sleep and that no one could force him to stay alive – that day, we could sense that he was in an extremely dangerous situation. He was falling apart, on the edge of a precipice, and had to be hospitalized.

Another aspect of his personality soon appeared: he would engage in all sorts of delinquent acts, provocations, perverted behaviour, and disrespect for the law of the land. These no doubt helped him to survive, as though they were simply part of a game. In the play scenarios that had this as their theme, he took pleasure both in being caught and threatened with prison, and in not being caught and therefore coming through with no harm done. It was like an attempt at feeling something at a particular moment in time that he was desperately trying to catch hold of, while at the same time seeming indifferent, with a kind of sexual non-differentiation.

One day, he began the session as he usually did – repeating that he had nothing to say and that, anyway, he knew that he never said anything. It then became possible, however, to get him to play out the painful silence and to represent the wall that cut him off from the rest of the world – a wall that would no longer be opaque, but would let things through in waves, given that there were henceforth some openings in it.

After about 18 months of psychodrama, there was a significant change in the tonality of what he was experiencing. In the background, there was a mother figure – absent, immature and burdened down with children – who had been unable to support him and pamper him. In the terror that Mr. Z could not express in words, that mother figure became connected with the birth of his own child. We played out scenarios that echoed this.

The fact of having nothing to say, silence, distress, depression and de-cathexis – all this said it for him, and above all manifested the persistence of a relationship that, to say the least, was unclear and ambiguous; a relationship that, with its presence/absence, connected him to the "incestuous" woman of his early adolescence. He showed that, in his thoughts, she had never let him go and that he neither wanted nor was able to leave her.

The absence of a mother figure, being deprived of her, was matched by the reality of a sexual act so early in life, by an intrusive and incestuous presence. Mr. Z thus had to freeze any sensations that he felt were too powerful, to come to a halt and paralyse the passing of time. It was his only chance of survival. For a long time, in the psychodrama sessions, we had to try to feel our way forward whenever we raised the subject. How could we play that character without, whether we wanted to or not, making something nostalgic out of it or – and this was more often the case – casting it against type and turning it more into a superego-like Other?

A woman who had given him some kind of existence, but who had both loved and destroyed him: the three terrifying attributes of an object that had become omnipresent and omnipotent and would never let him go. A woman, a ghostly object, neither alive nor dead, like a phantom haunting him, possessing him, getting mixed up with him and making it impossible for him to live other than in silence and absence. Just when Mr. Z seemed to be more present and more involved in the play scenarios, what he kept on saying was that he was living completely in her shadow.

That echoes what Freud wrote about "The Theme of the Three Caskets" in Shakespeare's *Merchant of Venice*: "the three forms taken by the figure of the mother in the course of a man's life – the mother herself, the beloved one who is chosen after her pattern, and lastly the Mother Earth who receives him once more" (1913, p. 301). In other words, the one who gives life, the one who loves, and the one who receives in death, i.e. who destroys. Instead of being different figures in the course of life, following each other as time goes by, for Mr. Z they were all mixed up together, short-circuiting temporality and making time come to a halt. For Mr. Z, there was no longer any possible "sense" – no direction, progressive or retrogressive, and no meaning, no reality.

We had to wait until some distance could intervene before Mr. Z, in the course of his psychodrama, could convey to us the extent to which he was in communication with a devitalized object, one that had no real consistency or presence other than in the kingdom of shadows. He lived in that shadowy area and locked himself up inside it so as not to sink into the void or become completely de-structured; but the risk was that he might be pushed out of it.

One day, in reply to the initial question – something of a ritual – as to how he was feeling, Mr. Z said that he did not feel well at all. There was a deep distress inside him that made him feel at a loss. He was asked to explain the difference between those two ideas, and try to be more precise about what was part of each of them. He then said that he could talk about that difference for quite some time, but that would imply psychotherapy – and that was the preserve of his analyst. In fact, he had remained almost silent during the previous three years of his psychotherapy; she had been very patient with him and he was grateful for that. He could now acknowledge that he was beginning to get to grips with that and that at last he would be able to say something. Then he went on: "As for the psychodrama, I don't quite know what I get out of it or what I do with what it gives me, but it certainly does give me something."

Although the difference he made between psychotherapy and psychodrama is at first glance quite vague, it would be well worth thinking about the way in which these particular techniques – both of which were offered to Mr. Z in parallel function – especially as regards what differentiates them and also the links between them. On the one hand talking, on the other play-acting. In his case there was probably a lot of internal devastation, emptiness and silence as far as the psychotherapy aspect was concerned, while in the psychodrama there was helplessness, distress and confusion. Two modalities, two loci that echoed each other and fitted into each other so as to build up ever so gradually an internal aspect where beforehand there was only emptiness and confusion, and to make some kind of relationship with the object bearable – in this case, the psychoanalyst whom Mr. Z felt to be dangerous, hence his immobilizing and neutralizing of her until that point.

It can happen that, in the course of psychoanalytic psychotherapy or psychoanalysis, a relentless repetition or deadly silence comes to the fore and takes hold of everything to such an extent that the continuation of the treatment is jeopardized. When psychodrama is set up in parallel to the analysis, this can often help to get round that difficulty – which has to do with phases of absolute coincidence, without any gaps or cracks, between different categories of time. Reduplicating the analytical situation in this way, with the setting up of two spaces and two time periods, may help the patient to move from one to the other and re-establish a temporality that had become locked into itself.

Mr. Z's situation was marked, inter alia, by an early form of collusion between excitation and enacted sexuality at a time when, psychologically immature and unable to take support from an infantile sexuality as yet unintegrated, he was unable to deal with it. The traumatic sexual experience brought him to a kind of blurring or immobilization. At best, there was a conjunction between idealization and death that prevented him from regressing – a collusion between time periods as he was developing and the collapse of psychical agencies in his mental organization, so that he remained mentally paralysed and insensitive to both internal and external stimulation.

As Ferenczi put it, "It is natural to compare this with the precocious maturity of the fruit that was injured by a bird or insect" (1949, p. 229). What he described as a "traumatic progression" creates a dichotomy with respect to infantile sexuality and indeed disqualifies, wipes out and nullifies sexuality. In Mr. Z's case, there was some degree of going beyond sexuality, but there was no indication of maturity or of the understanding of other people, which, as Ferenczi argued, are brought about in these particular circumstances.

Mr. Z took refuge in an immobilization of any kind of desire, in fantasying, a stasis between dream and delusion. He had to be pulled away from that area of illusion without putting him too much at risk because it was a crucial element for him. In order not to fall apart, his ego attached itself to a shadow that he could not let go of, to an object that was both a mother figure and a lover, devitalized, with no substance, diaphanous, inaccessible and impossible to take hold of – but one that kept him alive in an in-between situation, that kept him from sinking into oblivion. That was the paradox and the danger of the situation that he found himself in. What he felt to be a threat, something bursting in on him, was the violence and destructiveness that, in his view, any encounter that was too firmly anchored in reality must of necessity entail.

In what way could we attempt to draw closer to that zone of intangible confusion other than by bringing it face-to-face, within a particular setting, with the non-dangerous presence of human beings in their materiality, in the reality of their bodies and their differences? His psychoanalyst understood that perfectly, which is why she referred him to us for psychodrama; that would help him move from the evanescent and ethereal experience that he was having with her in his psychoanalytic sessions to the present moment of psychodrama in all of its concreteness.

At the heart of psychoanalytic psychodrama lies the idea of the "double"; it is this that, in the play scenario, enables us to present the patient with an incarnation of various possible options. For Mr. Z, one of the therapists became an object offering him some support – he would systematically choose that person who, depending on the scenarios that were being played out, let himself talk freely not only about ideals, dreams, disappointments, distress and hate, but also about food, women and ambition. This was therefore another possible "self" for Mr. Z, he who was unable to play any role other than his own. A narcissistic object, neither shadow nor fictitious, that set him on the road to identification. A "double" for himself, but one that was alive, one that helped him think of himself differently and whose vitality Mr. Z was able to take for himself.

Gradually, his attitude began to change. He became more "present", able to take on some degree of continuity, and from time to time managed to anticipate what was to be played out. He imagined two guitar players, one of whom would be playing in too mechanical a fashion without any feeling, while the other would be playing too emotionally. Mr. Z's progress was particularly evidenced by the fact that one day he said that he would like to meet in reality the woman who had seduced him. Facing up to reality was initiated thanks to the scenarios that were played out concerning that theme; the psychoanalytic psychodrama represented the locus where such a movement could take place.

The turning point came when Mr. Z, more and more aware of the reality effect brought about by the psychodrama, became able to see connections between one session and another. When he could anticipate the following session, he was able to acknowledge and accept the discontinuity that was part of its continuity. That was his way of demonstrating that the session had left inside him traces that were experienced both as belonging to reality and as memory traces, with the possibility of projection into the future.

Psychoanalytic psychodrama and traces of reality

It has often been said that psychodrama offers the opportunity for representing in a figurative way the patient's internal conflicts. It does this by encouraging representation in an attempt to give meaning to something that until then had none. The dream model was often taken as a template for psychodrama, so that this new technique could gradually come to be accepted and its credibility acknowledged when compared to psychoanalytic treatment as such. Here, however, something else is at stake: registering something that the patient has hitherto been unable to record – or, rather, something that keeps on being erased, paralysed or destroyed.

Psychodrama in such cases is the most appropriate technique for attempting to construct or to reconstruct, and perhaps to create, what keeps on slipping away, something that cannot be grasped. This has nothing to do with repression as such – not even with primary repression – but with deconstruction, falling apart, disruption.

Is it a question of rediscovering what has disappeared through being rubbed out or fragmented? Or rather one of identifying something that failed to be imprinted? How, in psychodrama, are we to think about external reality, a notion that, at least theoretically, plays no part in the classic form of psychoanalysis, where the focus is on psychical reality?

Insofar as the impossibility of topographical and temporal regression is a clear indication of the psychotic organization, can Freud's model be of any help to us? Freud showed that the primary processes linked to the satisfaction of internal needs in the pleasure–unpleasure system come up against reality-testing, with different kinds of transformation and adaptation; this evolves in the direction of a movement away from directly satisfying the body to putting on hold, via fantasy and play, the gratification of the sexual drives.

Psychodrama functions in the reverse direction – it takes support from external reality. To some extent – and this is no doubt something that puts off some psychoanalysts – it is characterized by the immediacy, rapidity and even violence that is part of external reality. It goes along with the defences, as they come to be adjusted and subverted within a strictly defined setting, so that what had never managed to be registered – or is no longer registered – can gradually come to be so, or once again come to be so.

Playing out scenarios and suggesting representations – is that all that has to be done to enable the patient to represent the other as well as his or her own self?

In the encounter between psychoanalysis and the cinema, analogies were made between these two kinds of experience and, from the 1970s on, were made the most of by theorists of cinematographic art. One approach was to use psychoanalysis as a model of criticism; this was applied to films by Eisenstein and by Hitchcock. Another idea was to draw a parallel between films and mental phenomena such as dreams. In a more sophisticated approach, the idea of an analogy between cinematography and the psychoanalytic setting, both of which are based on the same mechanisms as those which govern the construction of the ego, offers no doubt more refined possibilities – my intention here being to apply it not to the theory of the cinema but to psychoanalysis.

Psychodrama could be seen as analogous to cinematographic techniques insofar as the immediacy of projecting a film lets us grasp in a very perceptible and condensed manner – and one that is speeded up – a modality of organization and its transformations. What the psychoanalyst has to deal with when treating psychotic patients is a relationship that is set up, on the one hand, very quickly and massively, and, on the other, step by step, word by word, intonation by intonation, with several phases of starting all over again so that what appeared to be fixed, empty or a jumble of emotions and painful feelings can be allowed to emerge.

The word "technique" should be understood in its two meanings: as a set of mechanisms in the concrete, material sense, with their sensitivity (a roll of film has sensitivity); and as psychical mechanisms based on processes of splitting, idealization and identification.

The idea of the "fourth wall" employed by Oudart in the *Cahiers du Cinéma*, referring to the opening opposite which the film is projected onto the screen, is, in my view, well worth going back to and looking at again. Dubois (1990) describes it as that hypothetical space that never lets itself be seen and from which the scene is contemplated; this is the place the spectator occupies or, better, his imaginary representation. That has something to do with what psychotic patients experience, and it may help us to understand that experience better: anxiety that cannot be expressed in words or represented, facing a hypothetical space that opens onto absence, emptiness, chasm, nothingness. In that set-up, in place of absence, of the "fourth wall" that remains to be constructed, there is the presence of the psychoanalyst. The perceptual arrangement offers the patient, through the face-to-face relationship that is part of the encounter, an end-point to what can be seen, a "wall" – otherwise he or she would be looking into a void, emptiness – perhaps we could even say the possibility of putting things into perspective. Over and beyond the break with the object, the analyst in person is there, an external object that can be internalized; the analyst's watching eyes act like a camera, in a way similar to what Roland Barthes says in *Camera Lucida*. On being photographed, he wrote: "Now, once I feel myself observed by the lens, everything changes: I constitute myself in the process of 'posing', I instantaneously make another body for myself, I transform myself into an image" (Barthes, 1980 [1993, p. 10]).

In psychodrama, there is the physical presence of the group of therapists. It may to some extent satisfy the patient's exhibitionistic and voyeuristic impulses when these can be better tolerated; it may also encourage enactments of scenarios in which representations work at integrating, restructuring and translating elements that have not been taken in or processed. Psychodrama also offers the possibility of getting back in touch with sensory reality.

The issue, after all, is how to try to understand what is taking place as the patient moves out of his or her ghostly – not fantasy – world, and goes towards a more real world, one that is not experienced as dangerous. (As we saw in Mr. Z's case, his ghostly world, paradoxically, kept him alive.)

The importance of bodies that move around, come closer together then move apart, within a clearly defined spatio-temporal setting, the looks exchanged between those who are playing out the scenario and those who are watching – all this contributes, inter alia, to the strengthening of being-there, of presence, which aims to create reality traces thanks to which some registering and integration of present time can be accomplished. There is indeed a confrontation between "actual-ness" and the present in and through the play scenario, with the staging of a before and of an after.

The feeling of being "outside" of time and immobilized, as well as the excitation that is experienced are, in psychodrama, brought into the acting and present time of the play scenario. The feeling of being absent from one's body and the fuzziness of imagos are met with by the actual physical presence of the therapists. Similarly, missing memory traces are replaced by constructing "reality traces".

Here too, all the same, perception, external reality and conscious input – typical elements of psychodrama – are not enough for the patient to cathect what until then had not been cathected or to feel that he or she exists in a relationship with some other person.

Zapping implies making something appear then immediately disappear without trace. How are we to arrange things so that traces may once more be registered and preserved?

A lot of emphasis has been placed on the importance, in psychodrama, of sensory and perceptual reality, of looking at one another, of moving around and making various gestures – of everything, in short, that makes for presence in the here-and-now of the session. However, it is not direct contact with reality as such but only by means of that direct contact and through the discontinuity of times and places that another crucial alternation can be established, one which, within the technical setting, highlights the contrast between play and reality. In this way, processes of individuation and internalization can be set up.

As in the metaphor of the mystic writing-pad, psychodrama gives an important role to external stimuli in encouraging the perceptual apparatus to function again. Through its role as a protective shield against excitation, it must enable "effects of reality" to be set up through the use of discontinuity; in this way, both subject and object will be registered, each being indissociable from the other.

At the beginning and end of each session, before and after the chosen scenario is played out, patient and play leader have a discussion together. Psychodrama starts off with present time and reality and goes on to create, via its particular technique, traces of existence, traces of reality, replicas of the "memory traces" that psychotic anxieties no longer allow – or have never allowed – to be registered.

Unlike the classic form of psychoanalytic treatment, which to a greater extent leaves external reality aside, psychodrama takes it as its basis – but even here there is no direct effect of external reality on the patient. The essential factor is the gap between the play scenario and reality, so that "traces of reality" or "effects of reality" can be created, in the sense of setting up an innermost and lasting certainty that the world, human beings and the experiences that are being lived through are well and truly real. It is as though these patients had never, until then, been able subjectively to have that

certainty and thereby become themselves part of the unfolding of a process in which time itself has duration.

By inventing several possible versions, false causal explanations can be disentangled, those in which the starting point and the end-point are one and the same, such that they cancel each other out (or, sometimes, fill up a void). Above all, the multiplicity of versions that are put forward and coexist come from the subtle interplay between fiction and reality, thereby broadening the mental domain.

There are two main elements that make reality more tolerable within the psychodrama setting. One is that the transference is diffracted over several therapists. The other is the repeated experience in the course of the same session of an alternation between the multiplicity of times and spaces and the unity of the face-to-face discussion with the play leader (who does not participate in the actual playing out of the scenario), then again between unity and multiplicity every time that patient, therapists and play leader, each in turn, come together then separate. While patient and therapists focus on playing out the chosen scenario then come back to reality, the play leader does not participate directly – he or she is the guarantor of the patient's reality. That reality is not yet meaningful; it is different from the play scenario that can be made meaningful, once the necessary reality effect is sufficiently integrated, thereby opening up the possibility of thinking, dreaming and fantasizing.

In addition, this necessary continuity/discontinuity of time and place, of unity and multiplicity, of playing and reality is not simply a matter of alternation. It combines with the continuity/discontinuity of a *mise en abyme* structure (the play within the play), which means that differentiations based on the perspective and dynamics of showing/being shown and seeing/being seen become even more pronounced. There, too, something of the "Real" may lead to self-representation.

The model for this could be the *mise en abyme* construction that we find in *Hamlet*: inside the play that the theatre audience is watching, there is another play, the pantomime organized by Hamlet and watched by the characters of the main play. The aim is to reveal the scene that is kept hidden – we might almost say "repressed": the scene of treachery and of the murder of Hamlet's father. It is a way of creating a special space, a special perspective that makes possible a degree of depth, which, for example, is missing in the Magritte painting that I referred to earlier. Merleau-Ponty's analysis here is particularly apposite. In referring to Dutch paintings, when "an interior in which no one is present is 'digested' by the 'round eye of the mirror'," he says: "Artists have often mused upon mirrors because beneath this 'mechanical trick', they recognized, as they did in the case of the 'trick' of perspective, the metamorphosis of seeing and seen that defines both our flesh and the painter's vocation" (1961 [1964, p. 168–169]).

It is as though, starting from a flat, two-dimensional body image, it becomes possible for the patient, thanks to a particular sensory and perceptual setting, to rediscover (or perhaps even to register) traces of reality in order to "fabricate" an internal body image. In the hoped-for movement from a body that can feel to a body image, looking functions as a kind of physical touching; this is not perhaps the same thing as Winnicott described when he wrote of the mother's gaze resembling that of a mirror. The scenario that is being played out involves other things in addition to looking, but it does have its roots in a global bodily perception. That was what that patient felt when he said to me, session after session, that he did not come to talk to me but to see me. To that idea of "being-there", he might well have added: to be seen and to see each other, or again, to touch me, to be touched and to touch each other, in the same way as we pinch ourselves in order to be sure of the reality of what we are experiencing.

For patients who are cut off from their past, those to whom this new psychoanalytic experience is being offered, the important element is that they manage to be refocused, to be put in touch with their sensitivity and highlighted so that they become subjects in their own right. It is from exterior to interior that they can construct themselves, that their body can come alive, feel things, take shape. To return to the cinematographic analogy, the analyst's presence and looking works like a "photographic act", the effect of which is not to be a reproduction or representation of what is "real" but to carry within itself signs that constitute traces of reality.

PART THREE

The Vertigo of Creation

7

Liminal space, manic writing

Some patients have a kind of writing that I would call manic. It never stops, it involves only here-and-now "actual-ness" and it is an attempt at fighting against the gradual slipping away of the world. Trying to hold on to every moment and every detail through words is a way of preventing the world from falling apart. In order not to lose the world, not to lose oneself, the idea is to build up, without leaving any gaps, a kind of instantaneous memory, which, however, is ineffective and has forever to be started all over again. A sign of deep anxiety and an omnipotent attempt to hold and contain everything in one's grasp, this kind of writing blocks off all temporality, which is supplanted by the uninterrupted presence, inside a scriptural space, of oneself and of the world. It is based on the wish to control reality through meticulous and uninterrupted writing about what the external world might be; this is obviously just as much a defence against the external world as against the reality of the internal world – even more so, perhaps. It is, in fact, the opposite of any emerging of memories and of registration in a time that could constitute an origin, including a mythical one.

What, then, makes such an undertaking any different from that of some novelists? Where does the temptation lie? On the literary dimension for some patients and the manic one for some writers? Where does the dividing line lie? Deleuze (1993 [1997, p. 13]) put forward the very interesting idea according to which, "literature is delirium, but delirium is not a father–mother affair". With reference to Blanchot, he goes on: "literature begins only when a third person is born in us that strips us of the power to say 'I' (Blanchot's 'neuter')".

Psychotic patients do not have that recourse to otherness; all that they know about manic writing is that they need it and that it is painful. Laurence Sterne's *The Life and Opinions of Tristram Shandy, Gentleman* (1759) plays on the representation of manic writing and on the illusion of a work that is life; it helps us to explore more fully the notion of representation and to have a better idea of the experience of giving up and catching hold again of the life-work that is being created.

In his paper on "The Unconscious", Freud says that, in schizophrenics, there is a contradiction between the idea of the ego's attempts at flight, accompanied by a withdrawal into narcissism, and that of an increased cathexis of the ego. He writes:

> We might rather expect that the word-presentation, being the preconscious part, would have to sustain the first impact of repression. . . . This, it is true, is difficult to understand. It turns out that the cathexis of the word-presentation is not part of the act of repression, but represents the first of the attempts at recovery or cure.
> (1915b, p. 203)

Recovery? Cure? With his idea of the preconscious, as described in his topographical model, Freud is at the centre of the problem situation typical of the psychoses. It is indeed the case that the breakdown or falling apart that occurs in psychotic patients has nothing to do with repression. Verbal language and word-presentations, except in cases of mental deficiency or autism, are not in themselves affected; such patients tend rather, as our clinical experience shows us, to hyper-cathect the word-part, the word for the word's sake. This implies that their relationship to abstraction is somewhat paradoxical; we must therefore look again at what Freud says about the relationship between words and things in their dissociation. I would argue that, on the threshold of consciousness, there is something that I would call "liminal", manifested, among other situations, in some kinds of borderline writing.

The word-part and the liminal

Margaret Little's poem "Words" (1986), which she wrote while she was in analysis with Winnicott, describes the experience of being cut off from oneself. There are many other poems like that one, private poems written by psychotic patients or concentration-camp poems written just before the author's disappearance and destruction.

From what space do these words emerge? As we try to define the "ordinary writing" of patients and analyse the part it plays in their overall mental organization, we come up against the difficulty of finding the correct register in which to inscribe it.

The key role of linking together and communicating played by the preconscious governed by secondary processes is well known. Some have spoken of flaws in the preconscious, whereas here in fact it is hyper-cathected. This underlines the fact that the idea that these patients are very close to their unconscious – as has often been said to be the case – is unsustainable; nor is it possible to claim that their secondary processes fail in the task of holding back confusion and disorganizing excitation, so that these patients are functioning in a primary-process modality.

A detour via the metapsychological fiction is necessary here. From an economic point of view, in the representation that we can have of it, the disruption that occurs whenever there is a confrontation with reality cuts the individual off from his or her unconscious and overloads the preconscious. There follows a kind of loop functioning that makes for continuous repetition, an autonomous preconscious-consciousness (Pcs.-Cs.) circuit deprived of any bedrock in the unconscious and of any to-and-fro movement between the psychical agencies. That break changes the nature of the role of the preconscious; cut off from its foundations, it becomes a kind of rampart against emptiness and nothingness. That defensive modality is expressed either by turning away from any kind of feeling and being drawn towards the void in an attempt to control it better, or by an intensification of verbal language. The perceptual system is put off balance; the only way in which it can function is in terms of even more excitation, an overflow of internal feelings with too much stimulation coming from the external world.

The isolation of the Pcs.-Cs. system is expressed either by a hyper-cathexis of the preconscious (and therefore of language and verbal thinking) or, as a counter-reaction, by its inhibition. This emphasizes the break that has occurred with respect to the patient's infantile sexual past, with the ensuing impossibility of setting up any progressive or retrogressive movement (or at least a more or less important difficulty in so doing, depending on each particular case). The here-and-now of "actuality" is the dominant element in a space-and-time that always has to be reinvented. This is a qualitative leap, which is no doubt what Bion meant by his idea of "thoughts without thinkers".

Any challenge to the concepts of word-presentations and thing-presentations also implies a similar challenge – even though the issue would seem by now to be resolved – to a term that Freud soon abandoned. I am referring here to the much-discussed "subconscious". Freud abandoned the idea because he felt it would create confusion with respect to the unconscious.

André Breton is responsible for any potential confusion between these notions. Through practising what he called automatic writing, he thought that he could have direct access to the unconscious and be able to "catch hold of" it. Breton was fascinated by Freud, to such an extent, indeed, that he commented on Freud's work, imitated him or took issue with him – but Freud knew little of Breton. The misunderstanding that kept them apart, like their abortive meeting, must not lead us to neglect the experiences that the Surrealists attempted.

Following Rimbaud, they advocated a long, immense and reasoned unsettling of all the senses, something that would closely resemble a state of hallucination and creation. Aragon (1924) explains this in the following words:

> Everything happened as if the mind, having reached this confluence of the unconscious, had lost track of where it was pouring out. In it subsisted images that took form, that became the substance of reality. They expressed themselves according to this relation, in a perceptible form. They thus took on the character of visual, auditory, and tactile hallucinations.

The idea, through an experimentation that was not without risk, was to attain via "thought-writing" (Breton, 1963) lying beneath the threshold of consciousness, a state of derealizing disorganization of space and time that would "determine the precise constitution of the subliminal" (Breton, 1970 [1999, p. 129]). This was a vague zone, uncertain, unorganized, with all frontiers abolished between dreams and reality, between spoken and written language, between everyday language and poetry – a kind of reservoir of creation. Breton borrowed from Flournoy the idea of the "subliminal ego" (Flournoy himself had taken it from Myers) and cleared it of any spiritual aura. What Breton wanted to "catch hold of", thinking that he was dealing with the unconscious, had probably more to do with that locus which gave sustenance to feelings of the uncanny, one that the surrealist poets, refusing the idea of meaning and writing, liked to visit.

Distinct from the unconscious, that zone, which is situated beneath the threshold of consciousness, unorganized but occasionally productive, may well be the one in which our psychotic patients live. A place of non-contradiction, of non-differentiation between real and imaginary, between life and death, between past and future. This is what we come across in our clinical practice – not an access to the unconscious, but the revelation of an intermediate zone that resembles it, one that is made up of desires and chaos. It is an imitation of the unconscious, the simultaneous emanation and source of what could be seen as a "subliminal ego".

Patients try to emerge from that "subliminal" state – I prefer to call it "liminal" – through resorting to a limit-writing that aims, merely by naming, to recreate their existence with respect to themselves and to the world. It is as though the preconscious, which ordinarily plays a pivotal role in structuring, had become short-circuited, its only function being to name and its only support the word-part of the thing. This brings to mind Magritte's "word-paintings".

Therefore, in preference to Micheline Enriquez's term "representative writing", which lays more emphasis on the nature of that writing and especially on what becomes of it, I would suggest that we use the term "liminal writing", because this includes the idea of where it originates: on the threshold of consciousness, at the extreme limits of what lies close to disintegration and delusion. "Liminal" writing is not the result of any process; it is a recourse and its functions are many in number. Through its cathexis of sensorimotor activities and the setting-up of a new potential memory, it offers some protection against anxiety and facilitates a short-lived and fragile attempt to reunify the mind; that attempt has to be made again and again because there is no appropriate body image.

"Liminal" writing is one of survival. The Surrealists artificially reproduced the ego's disorganization, and in our patients reality becomes de-structured – but writing can put some order into all of this and recreate (or, rather, create) a reality that remains to be defined. It comes from the psychotic temptation.

It is in that space between life and nothingness, in that in-between experience, that some psychotic patients stand, in an apparent return – one that is forever being renewed – towards the "before" moment of conception, the "before" of things that have not yet come to pass. Their difficulty is that of accepting the materiality of a body in its finiteness, i.e. with an end, an afterwards and above all a "time-before". The written words that they create offer them an immediate but temporary support, one that is crucial whenever their ego trembles or dissolves. Liminal writing has nothing to do with any process of working-through. It is an original piece of work, a pure creative impulse, which, in a paradox that belongs exclusively to it, marks out a narcissistic flaw and an attempt at its cicatrization.

It might seem obvious that the idea of sublimation should enter the picture at this point. That, however, would open up too wide a domain, one that is very badly defined in psychoanalytic texts. Is it really suitable for describing an activity that calls upon a necessity that is simultaneously modest, obscure and essential, one that has no roots in unconscious wishes but comes from something that is cut off? The creation of an artefact that is not the outcome or the rerouting of a drive impulse – indeed, it denies the drives and blocks them off.

The generic term "sublimation", which evokes a symbolic dimension of "top" and "bottom" as Freud (1910) describes it in *Leonardo da Vinci and a Memory of his Childhood*, does give rise to some confusion. "Top" and "bottom" refer explicitly to sexuality and to a representation of the genitals and sexual functions. "The pride and hope of human beings" (1910, p. 97) in the earliest times of human civilization, and therefore at the highest point in any hierarchy of values, sublimation gave rise to innumerable divinities, writes Freud. In contemporary society, the genitals are culturally disparaged, and therefore pushed to the bottom as objects of shame and repression. Somewhat ambiguously, sublimation seems to be less of an elevation than a diversion of sexuality, a stratagem that brings out other moral and ascetic values.

The return to the notion of the Sublime, throughout the eighteenth century, may shed another, more fruitful light on the concept that Freud proposed. For Burke, terror is the first principle of the sublime.

> Whatever is fitted in any sort to excite the ideas of pain, and danger, that is to say, whatever is in any sort terrible, or is conversant about terrible objects, or operates in a manner analogous to terror, is a source of the sublime.
>
> (1909–1914, p. 20)

Perhaps another meaning could be given to the contrast between top and bottom – in terms of a psychical construction with its deficiencies and splittings that function as glass ceilings.

An artist is someone who takes hold of reality and makes it correspond to his or her vision of things. The poet does not submit to the values of society, contrary to what claims of sublimation all too often would have us believe; he or she subverts them in the assumption of freedom. Poets make use of language to deviate it from its usual meaning and constraints, and in so doing they set free the word-part. With their ability to let go of themselves, they manage to use words that arise in the liminal space, as a copy of the unconscious, in order to re-create them. Sublimate, not deviate, but refine and transform through a subtle chemical operation oflanguage.

In that quest – or a sometimes short-lived attempt – the fact of resorting to words, to written words, implies both a loss of identity and a step towards an identity regained. The fear that is part of the writer's dilemma – the choice between living or writing or perhaps even between writing and undertaking analysis – expresses what is at stake in each of these activities in the quest for one's identity.

That is the paradox, perhaps, of writing in the psychoanalytic relationship: creation or artefact, necessary – and sometimes crucial – time or a superfluous one? It was crucial for one particular patient who, faced with the enigma of her existence, was interested only in photos and in words; she spent hours leafing through dictionaries. Superfluous for another patient who peppered the course of his analysis with all sorts of private writings, acknowledging that the interpreting activity of the analyst meant that he gradually had less and less need to do so.

A path, a time when some people can take hold of themselves, the creation of an artefact that can give support – writing in its materiality, linked to feelings of emptiness and of the terror that goes with it, can take on different forms, depending on the level of mental structuring. It may come from a fear of destruction, of having been emptied; it may be the trigger for that fear or perhaps even put an end to it. Basically, there is some fragility, a narcissistic flaw that this particular detour, when it is not blocked off, can enable the person involved to overcome. But there is always the impression of something that has not been "thought out" and "worked through".

More than splitting – which presupposes a coherent alternative system – we should be thinking, as we have seen, in terms of some defect or flaw that has occurred in infancy or beyond, of some disruption or breakdown in adolescence, leaving the individual in the grip of chaos or on the edge of a precipice, where the psychotic temptation lies. The relationship to words, and more particularly to written words, has to be taken into account as to its involvement in the disruptive effects that are present in this kind of functioning, effects that may bring about rifts in the ego.

Freud did not put forward any explicit theory of language, but, as we are well aware, the difference between words and things appears very early on in his thinking – no later, in any case, than 1891, when he wrote *On Aphasia*. His study of aphasia, on the cusp of neurology and psychology, was written when the idea of association came to him, in the shape of a comparison that set him on the road to working out a model of the psychical apparatus. The fibres reaching the cortex are compared to the letters of the alphabet contained in a poem with multiple associations. Aphasia, then, involves various disorders concerning links of representation or associations of words and objects.

Thing-presentations belong to the Ucs. (Unconscious) system, while word-presentations have to do with the Pcs.-Cs. system. In hysteria, the body expresses words the meaning of which is repressed. Freud argued that in any system what is first affected is what is the least organized, i.e. the most recent element – here, words. In his paper on "The Unconscious" (1915b), he says that he was somewhat put out when he realized that the model that he had constructed could not be applied to schizophrenic patients; against all expectations, they go on cathecting word-presentations, with the relationship to words taking precedence over the relationship to things. He had thought that this preconscious element would have been the first to be subjected to the impact of repression.

Several consequences that Freud found important follow on from that. In particular, he had to look again at the mechanism of repression and this led him to discover, in the psychoses, that of the denial of reality. Also, a distinction had to be made between unconscious representations that are made up solely of thing-presentations and conscious representations that contain both thing-presentations and word-presentations. He put forward the fundamental idea according to which

> our mental activity moves in two opposite directions: either it starts from the instincts and passes through the system *Ucs.* to conscious thought-activity; or, beginning with an instigation from outside, it passes through the system *Cs.* and *Pcs.* till it reaches the *Ucs.* cathexes of the ego and objects.
>
> (1915b, p. 204)

If that second direction remains open "to some extent", as he puts it, in the neuroses, the demands, both internal and external, that psychotic patients have to deal with mean that they do not have enough psychical space at their disposal, given all the splittings – and even more so the disruptions – that occur when they feel threatened by what Freud called "instigations" coming from outside. Afraid of being completely taken over, they function in the immediacy of a world that is slipping away from them, with the fear that they will lose their very substance and be erased.

As Freud suggested, in spite of his surprise, since the path that comes from or leads to the unconscious is to a considerable degree blocked off, we have to understand that psychotic patients "find themselves obliged to be content with words instead of things" (1915b, p. 204); they have to take support from these words and hold on not to their sound – this would still be too exciting – but to their visual and material aspect.

Here, words are not linked to things as in the normal functioning of consciousness and the preconscious. Words do not "replace" things, as we all too often hear it said, in a kind of equivalence – or, rather in a confusion between words and things. What occurs is a dissociation – not an equating – between words and things in which only the word-part is retained. That way of seeing the situation leads to a quite different apprehension of the psychotic way of being.

Given all the disruptions that occur, the word-part is the only support available. When there is confusion, words take on too much meaning, given the excessive nature of the excitation; or they may be emptied of all meaning through the fear of destruction, such that language becomes disconnected from any registration in the perceptual or corporeal modes. Words, then, no longer mean what they usually do; they are signs.

This is probably what Freud meant when he said that "the cathexis of the word-presentation . . . represents the first of the attempts at recovery or cure" (1915b, p. 203). That is undoubtedly one solution.

We could perhaps see them as fetish-words, but not as Freud described fetishes in "Splitting of the Ego in the Process of Defence" (1940b [1938]), i.e. linked to a denial of castration, although Freud did see that process as being specific to the psychoses. Here, quite another element comes into play, one in which trickery has no role – one in which words, and more often than not written words, the work of survival, are the only possible recourse when certain devastating experiences occur.

Unlike the pleasure that the mind can take, which, as Freud describes it in *Jokes and Their Relation to the Unconscious* (1905a), depends on the cathexis of a preconscious thought brought down to an unconscious thought and thereby setting reason free, the mind of psychotic patients is usually imprisoned inside a kind of thinking based on reasoning, because the unconscious has an abundance of images whereas the preconscious handles words, word-parts. Words to which one can cling, words that are imitations of images? Often abstract images of fragmentation, catastrophe or death.

Manic writing

Timon, who was in his thirties, had always filled up notebooks in which he wrote down in detail what he was doing and what was going on around him, hour by hour – and sometimes even minute by minute – with so much precision that it all seemed both reassuring and pointless. A manic writing that nothing could stop.

In his remarkable description of the act of writing, Maurice Blanchot writes of "tyrannical prehension". He sees in it a pathological act.

> The writer's mastery is not in the hand that writes, the "sick" hand that never lets the pencil go – that can't let it go because what it holds it doesn't really hold; what it holds belongs to the realm of shadows, and is itself a shade. Mastery always characterizes the other hand, the one that doesn't write and is capable of intervening at the right moment to seize the pencil and put it aside. Thus mastery consists in the power to stop writing, to interrupt what is being written, thereby restoring to the present instant its rights, its decisive trenchancy.
>
> (1955a [1982, p. 25])

Timon was a brilliant young man, with a whole string of qualifications. He had never been able to work and had no explanation for the gap that had rapidly opened up between his youthful ambitions, justified as they were, and the mediocrity of his everyday life. There was no possible access to his past, and he could not understand what, in his late teens, seems to have been a mental breakdown. The few elements pertaining to his past that he could relate were repeated without any conviction as to what he was saying; indeed, he spent little time on these simple facts, which, once he had recalled them, could not be taken any further or be linked up with anything else. Just the facts: a brother born when Timon was six years old, the death of his mother while he was still a teenager. His admiration for his father knew no bounds – idealized, his father was the only person who found favour with him. Timon kept him in slavery, as it were, whereas he hated terribly, and almost uncontrollably, all the other people whom he knew. In some ways, as long as that hatred lasted it connected him strongly with other people and prevented him from becoming severely depressed, having a breakdown, or being hospitalized (as indeed he had been several times).

Shortly after the start of his psychotherapy, Timon gave me his notebooks to read because, as he put it, they would teach me all that I needed to know about him. In fact they revealed nothing about him – they contained none of his own thoughts, reflections or feelings. They mentioned places, facts, gestures in their instantaneous aspect, transcribed at the very moment in which they were carried out; the monotony of everyday things, page after page, appallingly trite, completely uninteresting, with no affects, no depth. An omnipresence, a hyper-presence, unlike patients who write down lists, as in Micheline Enriquez's descriptions, for example – at least lists reflect back some part of reality and provide a solid base that those patients can cling to. In Timon's case, the reverse was the case: a hyper-presence in which the presentation, with its overly compulsive and exalted quality, came close to dissolving the ego. A Sisyphean task, an impossible coinciding between what was written and what ought to have been experienced, to the extent that, in this frenzied undertaking, both reality and life itself lost all construction. Paradoxically, however, it protected Timon from breakdown and delusion.

With his ego both threatened with being erased and abnormally enlarged, in constant expansion, Timon thought of himself as an example. At one point, he wanted to have his notebooks published so as to allow the world at large to benefit from his exceptional expertise – this cannot but remind us of Schreber. He contacted a friend of his who would help him to finalize the presentation of his manuscript based on his notebooks and make a book out of them. That friend, however – an object first of admiration, then of hostility – was soon pushed aside, especially when he advised Timon not to send the far from perfect initial draft of his manuscript to any publisher. For Timon, the project might have proved beneficial, helping him to look at himself so that he could stand back a little and enable some reflexivity to enter the picture; but the immediacy in which he lived could not allow a slow and difficult task to be carried through to a successful conclusion. As soon as the first rough draft was ready, he decided that the task of preparing the manuscript was already over. His friend was sent packing. The construction was supposed to be imposing, grandiose – yet it was painfully empty and had more to do with the shoring up of a building erected on shaky foundations.

It was his megalomania that prevented that project from getting anywhere near a personal and private quest. Cut off from what Proust called his "deep self", Timon was unable to create any kind of life-book, no matter how modest. We are far from what Barthes called "life writing" with reference to Proust, from the life of an author that could in itself be his complete works, in which writing is a radical practice. In *The Past Recaptured*, Proust described that as being an integral part of one's inner life. Towards the end of that book, he wrote:

> As for the inner book of unknown symbols (symbols carved in relief they might have been, which my attention, as it explored my unconscious, groped for and stumbled against and followed the contours of, like a diver exploring the ocean bed), if I tried to read them no one could help me with any rules, for to read them was an act of creation in which no one can do our work for us or even collaborate with us. How many for this reason turn aside from writing!
>
> (1927 [1970, p. 139])

Timon did not have any opening towards the mental space that he required in order for both stages on which his writing took place – the inner one and the material one – and for both categories of time – that of living and that of writing – to be differentiated from each other, respond to each other, correspond with each other.

The life-writing of Tristram Shandy: a blank page

If both categories of time seem to merge together in Laurence Sterne's novel, *The Life and Opinions of Tristram Shandy, Gentleman* (1759 [2003]), this is because the author, with a mixture of irony, derision, burlesque and absurdity, goes to the furthest limits of the part of madness that is present in every creation, the part that remains uncreated.

Laurence Sterne's description of the writer Tristram Shandy's mad attempts to abolish the notion of representation makes for pleasant reading. By making his life-work and his whole life correspond exactly to each other, Tristram Shandy wants both to challenge and to deny the question of origins. Who among writers has never felt the wish to write the ideal book, the unique, complete one that would contain all the others that have ever existed, would quote from them, summarize them, incorporate them and stand higher than all of them put together?

Sterne's novel could be described as the story of an author who-creates-himself-by-writing-a-book-about-himself-creating-himself. A kind of tautology or self-generation through thinking and writing.

Far from being a "story-teller", to borrow Todorov's term in his study of the *Thousand and One Nights*, the author, Tristram Shandy, in an equation between book and life, presents himself very differently. For Scheherazade, one has to tell stories in order not to die; in this way the orality of the narrative sets up and preserves otherness – a relationship with another person in which dependence and control both exist, with the fable being the instrument of survival.

With a metaphor taken literally, in which the production of a book is taken to be the same as giving birth to a child, Sterne puts forward the idea of an equivalence – indeed, a complete correspondence or symbolic equation – between life and writing. A mad and omnipotent undertaking that is constantly doomed to disillusionment – but it is pushed to its outer limits, in a denial of temporality and of logical reality. Tristram Shandy's life and opinions are thus to be seen not so much as an autobiographical or romantic reality but as an assertion that the book that is being written is nothing other than life and thoughts, just as there can be no life and no thoughts other than the book.

The only thread to follow here is that of writing in its various digressions – an endless, breathtaking race the aim of which is the absolute yet unachievable coincidence between writing and life. In the denial of sexuality and of temporality, the concept of representation is called into question, to the benefit of that of creation.

It is true, of course, that every literary production is specific in itself. Often, nonetheless, it will evoke some questioning as to the vertigo, the time of its creation that is difficult to define, to keep hold of, to describe and to go beyond. The creator, who lets him- or herself be taken by surprise, cannot but wonder about the mystery of the act of creation in which originated both the literary production and the creator him- or herself. An astonishing questioning that lies at the very heart of that production – sometimes it takes the form of a mirror image of the creator searching for his or her identity, sometimes it is the reflection of the process of creation by representing the artist and his or her avatars, or again it may be, in contemporary literature, like a work of art that mirrors itself and ends up by losing its own image through the interplay of construction/deconstruction.

From that point of view, the ambition to be omnipotent, which is that of the author/narrator, Tristram Shandy, is accompanied by moments in which his ego is erased – cf. the famous blank pages: blank, enigmatic, free from any inscription, the blank of certain chapters or the chapter that is missing.

Tristram Shandy's gamble is to make the moment of writing, that of reading and that of living coexist, come together and be immobilized – temporality is thus perfectly under his control, and everything takes place in the absolute here-and-now of "actualness". His life-work will not be a transcription or a representation of reality, it will be pure creation. To deny that aspect, that ambition to create a reality of writing – or to play it down – implies thinking of that life-work in terms of representation with respect to an external reality that it is attempting to reproduce, to reconstruct and to restore.

In such a context, the status that we give to reality is decisive for our reading of the author's work. We can see it as the assertion of a particular kind of representation, à la Sterne as it were. This would nonetheless still be a representation, which, composed of constructed signs, things and words, has some connection with the external world; it invokes senses and perceptions. The other possibility, focusing on certain elements of the text itself, including the blank pages, is that we see in it a reverse process of creation via the possibility of non-representation.

The constraints of sexuality – sometimes denied, sometimes mocked – come up against the omnipotence of an author who, in a gesture of involution and of moving freely backwards in time, creates his own genitors, witnesses his own conception and can even say of himself, outside of any chronology, "for my own part, . . . I am not yet born: – I have just been able, and that's all, to tell you when it happen'd, but not how; – so that you see the thing is yet far from being accomplished" (Chapter 1. XIV).

Given its permanent nature, it is obvious that "how" is the crucial question here – how does a child appear – but in this case it is intimately related to the question of how a book materializes.

By denying time, by denying sexuality seen either as mythological, mythical and the prerogative of the gods (Jupiter and Leda at the beginning of the book, Jupiter and Europa at the end) or as shameful and fit only for animals, Tristram Shandy does not belong to the real world, one that is acknowledged as such and accepted. Faced with mystery, he exists only through his omnipotent will to create himself and the world.

It is important to explore further the idea of dematerialization. The book, in fact, does not appear as an object in all of its materiality. It is manic writing from start to finish, as immaterial as a thought, which, in the same way, creates a transient world that is always being renewed, always in upheaval. It puts the question again and again, in an obsessive way because what is at stake is the very identity and existence of the person who is writing, the question of origins. For Tristram Shandy, the book *is* life. For the reader, it is a tension between creation and representation that never reaches fulfilment – or, particularly with respect to the blank pages, a tension between creation and non-creation.

Through that incessant question about origins – in which are mixed together in a confused way, even though differences are put to the test as the writing continues, the origins of life and those of a book – Laurence Sterne evades the choice suggested by Marthe Robert (i.e. between "bastard" and "foundling") that lies at the heart of Romantic art. Tristram Shandy, who was conceived perfectly legitimately, asks the question: when does the beginning begin? *Ab ovo*? The reference to Leda is there only for it to be wrongfooted: the story that is yet to come is a mythical narrative, a genesis, that intends to hold sexuality up to ridicule and abolish time – the twofold foundation of the human condition.

In this simultaneous bringing-together of the writer's work and life, an absurd example – which mocks the time of child prodigies beginning their life-work on the very day that they are born – there is a calculation that is worth noting. In terms of an obvious arithmetic based on insane premises, Tristram Shandy, as author, would need to live 364 times more quickly in order to make up, by writing, the time that he has lost. Yet, as Tristram Shandy explains, that gap can never be filled, the difference can only get bigger and the dissociation become more pronounced. Hence the absurd yet disturbing formula for this speeded-up race in which the more one writes, the more one has to write:

> As at this rate I should just live 364 times faster than I should write – It must follow, an' please your worships, that the more I write, the more I shall have to write . . . I shall never overtake myself whipp'd and driven to the last pinch.
>
> (Chapter 2, XVLIII)

The other possibility would be to write twelve books a year, which, at best, would mean only a one-day lead. A megalomaniac project, the illusion of creative liberty – but above all the avowal of a gap, of a dissociation of the ego in anyone who would like to see both lives, the life that is lived and the Romantic one, unfold at the same rhythm.

The collusion between life and writing, between life-work and author, by calling temporality and exteriority into question, makes any representation of reality impossible. Tristram Shandy, who in the novel is the author, gives no representation of the world. He does not depict it – his ambition is to make it come forth, as he himself, through writing, comes forth. Every character, every happening, every reference appears as an emanation, a creation of the author's thinking. It is the "verbal thinking" of the Surrealists.

Through writing, free-flowing thinking carries the writer along, fascinating him even inside his world that is both enclosed and infinite: "my pen, – it governs me, – I govern not it" (Chapter 3. XLIX). Denial of temporality goes hand in hand with the destruction of the narrative to the benefit of the only possible construction, that of the whimsical freedom of thinking. It combines with the megalomaniac project of "saying everything", as a liberation or creation of thinking by writing. A demand for freedom, but also for the confusion that disrupts the logical succession of chapters. The threat of erasing the self, of making it unsteady and disintegrating it, which feeds into the monomania of writing, becomes stronger and stronger, so that the narrative itself becomes contradictory and chaotic.

The mystery of sexuality, the mystery of thinking, riddles and mysteries – words that Tristram Shandy often writes. The mystery, inter alia, of the blank page, the enigma of woman, that "mysterious labyrinth of love" of which there is no definition – for Tristram Shandy, it is merely a word, with no idea to which it could be attached.

Literary criticism usually sees in blank pages something to do with an ideal, with inhibition, with exhaustion or even with destruction; but in its presence/absence does it not take on the value of something uncreated, a question about what is without having been?

Deleuze's idea of literature as a delusion is a thought-provoking one and is well worth taking up again. Being delusional means being dispossessed of oneself and creating a neo-reality that is outside of reality and in denial of reality; it is outside of time, outside of space, outside of context. Often those are the conditions required – and the price that has to be paid – if the act of writing, between idealization and annihilation, is to take place. The writer makes his language delusional by putting it outside the self even though it comes through a narrative of the self; this favours the capacity to create, to create with language and by means of language. When that capacity is lacking, thinking goes blank, like the blank page that constitutes a breach in the fantasy of self-generation.

It may well be, then, that the blank page in Tristram Shandy's novel does not represent a vision or an absence; it may be condensing within itself and only within itself, in its apparently ideal perfection and materiality, the turmoil and the vertigo, which, under the guise of well-presented fun and fantasy, come close to the mystery of the uncreated.

With its presence/absence, it may make that member of the clergy think of the mystery of the Divine, of the uncreated in the religious or perhaps delusional sense of the term: something that exists without having been created.

The fascination is not for the negative but for what does not yet exist – the child/book yet to be born, to be created, to be written – which both displays and preserves something that, in writing, is incomprehensible and impossible to put into words. No doubt this has to do with the fascination about and control over an experience of emptiness, of the void that every mystic knows – as do some writers, although in their case it is circumscribed by the dimensions of a page in a book, lying inside its limits as a kind of safeguard. As if there were an infinite unfolding of a game of loser-takes-all: against fiction, writing; against writing, the uncreated; against the uncreated, nothingness.

8

The delusional temptation and imaging thinking

In his reply to Pontalis, in 1982, when he was asked to write an article on thought disorders, Maurice Blanchot quoted Georges Bataille: "It is fear that carries me along, fear of what is at stake in the totality of thinking." He went on: "Fear . . . yes fear, which only limitless thinking can attain . . . but fear of what? The answer fills the universe, it fills the universe and it fills me: obviously, the fear of *Nothingness*" (Blanchot, 1982, p. 356)

It is precisely that which some of our patients whose mental organization is psychotic make us feel. They are caught in an extreme way between the nothingness and the limitlessness of thinking – just as, no doubt, some poets and artists are. Between nothingness and limitlessness lies, of course, everything that is possible and all of the vertigo, not only of creation but also of delusions.

Through his reading of Schreber's autobiography – with its questioning of filiation and origins, and its wish to be edifying for the world – Freud was able to confirm his theory of origins and of repression. In the quest which is that of psychotic patients, however, with their disorders of temporality, the issue of filiation is very much called into question – to such an extent, indeed, that filiation in itself is denied and gives rise, in the absence of any differentiation between beginning and end, either to being drawn towards something that has to do with origins, an unattainable primary unity, or to running away from the threat of a catastrophe that is yet to come. Nor is there any firm boundary between mythical or imaginary filiations, between mythological or religious beliefs and original conceptions that are those of the individual him- or herself. Sometimes, when all genealogy is relinquished, the only recourse left is that of self-generation – or, rather, when faced with the risk of giving up the self, that of auto-creation of the self and of the world.

In response to this, the relationship with the analyst may appear to offer a kind of originating, a beginning, an encounter that has as yet not been experienced, a two-person creation.

Faced with such vertigo in the test that is the clinical situation, Bion's suggestion may indeed be of some help. In discussing patients who carry out "attacks on linking" or who, more generally, are inclined to destructiveness, he argues that "The finite is 'won from the dark and formless infinite' " (1967 [1984, p. 165 – quote marks in original]). In this way, we can argue in favour of the need for an intermediate form of thinking and suggest, linked to the "liminal", the idea of "imaging" thinking. A "poetic" kind of thinking that creates images and serves as a relay for the delusional temptation; it gives shape to whatever is shapeless, and offers itself as an intermediary in the all-or-nothing of thinking.

Filiation and "non-generating"

At the crossroads of every attempt at solving the enigma of the presence of man and of the world – of man in the world – there is always, argued Freud, a family romance, in its widest sense, like that of the primal horde. Human beings in a line of descent that is more or less acknowledged, more or less accepted, together with the fantasies to which it gives rise.

Anyone who does not want to be caught up in the vertigo of going back in time, pulled towards an elusive primal moment, has to define in some way a primeval instant, a beginning. Freud suggested a theory of origins that took into account a global and coherent vision of humankind. Even more explicitly, in his discussion of nature and nurture, he wrote in a footnote to his paper on "The Dynamics of Transference": "Incidentally, one might venture to regard constitution itself as a precipitate from the accidental effects produced on the endlessly long chain of our ancestors" (1912, p. 99). That vision, which never stopped haunting him, lies at the very roots of psychoanalysis and of the idea of origins; it is one of the modalities of an originating that is impossible to think about but is always being questioned, whether individual or group-based. It is helpful here to draw a distinction between originating, evocative of a more vague and indeterminable beginning, and an originary that refers to a locus, to a thing or to fantasies that could be described as primary (Perron, 2003).

In a comment on the last text that he wrote, *Moses and Monotheism. Three Essays* (1939 [1937–1939]), Freud did not hide the difficulty that he found himself in when he attempted to reconstruct a well-founded history. He then turned towards poetical reality: "Where there is an unbridgeable gap in history and biography, the writer can step in and try to guess how it all happened" (Letter from Freud to Arnold Zweig, May 12, 1934).

In working with psychotic patients, the analyst may at times have a highly disembodied representation of family relationships – this may even give rise to the feeling that what is being said relates to personae rather than to people, and even less to parental imagos in Freud's meaning of the term. The isolation and profound loneliness in which some patients live, because of the fear of the object that holds them in its grip, have something to do with their description of the many parent-figures that invade their mind; in reality, they keep these at arms' length to avoid the stain of incest, and in so doing short-circuit any possible processing of the Oedipal situation. All family relationships are reprehensible and must be rejected. It is better not to have any at all, to be alone in the world and to be in touch with the omnipotence of self-creation.

For those who live in the horror of sexuality and reproduction, the various forms of genealogy – real, imaginary or delusional, depending on the patient's reflexivity and firm belief – can paradoxically be both a suture and a fracture. Usually in delusions, genealogy denies the specifically human and carnal element that exists in all filiation; it relates to the Divine – the patient can therefore avoid being abandoned in nothingness. Schreber was the recipient of divine rays – thus denying and nullifying the very idea of filiation. Freud, of course, spurning the texture and tonality of the delusion of origins, interpreted this in terms of a repressed homosexual fantasy.

One patient could not think of his parents without seeing a hole in which he felt he might be engulfed; he gave a description of an upper middle-class family, whose members were brilliant but had fallen from grace, were mad or deeply depressed, and who had quarrelled over money. Did he really see himself as belonging to a line of descent, a filiation? When he spoke of his family, was this not rather an example, via projections, of the construction of an imaginary genealogy in which parent-figures were elevated to the status of a myth, in the grandeur of destruction? For that patient, who deliberately placed himself outside all that as though he were a mere spectator, family gatherings were like an assembly of zombies, with each one in his or her own little bubble that excluded any possibility of an encounter with the others. He felt that the members of his family were strange; they were strangers to him, just as he was a stranger to himself.

In the course of her analysis, another patient gradually came to speak about having been raped when she was still an infant. Faced with what for her was the outer limit of what she could tolerate, she was trapped between her inability to process that event in fantasy and her firm belief that it was an unbearable reality. In that space where every danger lay, the procession of stealing and raping characters who appeared on the scene deprived her of any possibility of becoming part of a genealogy that was not delusional – and which would become threatening if that delusion began to crumble.

In such cases, notions of filiation and self-generation take on a very specific function, which, dominated by violence, belongs to the order of the created and the uncreated. Antonin Artaud was even more radical in his repudiation of any kind of genealogy or filiation. Contemptuous of the Divine, in "Here Lies", in his attempt to destroy language, he expresses the horror he feels at his own body, at the very idea of begetting and at the abjectness of both of these.

> I, Antonin Artaud, am my son, my father, my mother,
> And myself; leveller of the imbecile periplum where begetting is entangled:
>
> The periplum daddy-mummy and infant,
>
> Soot from the arse of the grandma, much more than from father-mother.
> Meaning that before mummy and daddy,
> Who, it is said, had neither father nor mother
> Anyway, where would they have got them . . .

Beforehand, this improbable hole
That the spirit tries to find for us,
To disgust us a little more with ourselves,
Was this useless body . . .

(Artaud, 1974, p. 77)

But does this imply self-generation? It is more like an absurd circular periplum, which, in the upheaval of temporality, makes Artaud say, a few lines later:

For it is the end that is the beginning,
And this end
Is the one
That does away with
Every means.

(Artaud, 1974, p. 84)

When Racamier (1989) quotes the initial lines of "Here Lies" in his introduction to *Antoedipe et ses destins* (*Antoedipus and its Vicissitudes*), his aim is to highlight the importance of the idea of self-generation in the psychoses. The term itself, however, which contains the idea of generation or begetting, albeit of oneself, reflects a certain ambiguity, in the sense that it does imply some kind of filiation, even though it may be reversed.

As we have seen, the quest for origins, whenever there is some distortion of temporality, does not lead to a fantasy of self-generation, but to a blurring, a confusion between beginning and end. This is what Racamier describes as a wish for non-generation or non-begetting.

With regard to the backwards movement that psychoanalysis operates, Racamier describes this as a movement from a primitive to a pre-object stage and then to one where there is no object. That is why the idea of Antoedipus is a necessary one, at the junction between object-related and narcissistic, between life and non-life. Racamier argues that this concept is a fundamental pattern in human beings at the origins of the ego, of the object and of the world. Antoedipus and Oedipus are to be seen as two lineages, not with one following on from the other but with their paths crossing and re-crossing. Also, the moderate form of the Antoedipus situation can adapt to the idea of the unity of the ego based on primal fantasies, whereas in the pathological form of that situation it is the denial of origins that is uppermost.

The idea of a fantasy emanating from the unconscious and linked to the lifting of repression is not part of Racamier's theory. He suggests the notion of fantasy/non-fantasy, which lies either in a forward-moving eventuality as a possible pre-fantasy, or, in a retrogressive way, as a movement back to non-differentiation. Fantasy/non-fantasy is defined by what it is not – as "something that is not the truth nor reality nor a delusion nor a fantasy nor a dream" (Racamier, 1992, p. 139). It is not capable of mobility (as in a scenario), or of connections and movement, or of transformation and working-through (p. 148). Racamier makes a distinction here between the fantasy of self-generation and unconscious primal fantasies; in addition, we can see how in the development of his thinking the concept of fantasy leads to that of fantasy/non-fantasy.

Might it not be more appropriate to see these patients as attempting not only to create the world and themselves *ex nihilo*, but also, with a view to complete domination, to suppress it and destroy themselves? We would then be in a better position to appreciate the extreme situation in which some psychotic patients find themselves. Given the more or less dramatic disruption to which their ego is subjected – on the edge of a precipice or of chaos – there is no other way of being: the delusional temptation of a "non-begetting".

I would argue that Schreber was in a state in which generating or begetting was impossible. Writing is a second-phase event and an attempt at reorganization, because, as we have seen, a written text puts its seal on what remains uncertain; it is the quest for that point in the original catastrophe that he called "memorial events". A fragmented text, often incoherent but sometimes dazzling and illuminated, in which language is maltreated. Terms like filiation and genealogy try to fill in the unthinkable nature of the "torturing" experience, of staggering unsteadily on the edge of a precipice. A creation emanating from what Schreber, mixing up the words, called "coitus with oneself"; in reality, it was an enclosing, a "non-generation".

The delusional temptation

To talk in terms of a delusional temptation rather than of a delusional solution is now becoming more common, and it enables us to take into consideration the various forms that delusional thinking – or thinking that is almost but not quite delusional – can take. It also implies that the boundary that separates delusional thinking from other kinds – and from poetic thinking in particular – is an uncertain one, one that is inherently mobile. Behind all of these kinds of thinking lies the fundamental and always enigmatic question that human beings evoke – the origins and meaning of life, of oneself, of the world – as well as the many attempts to answer it, either in part or as a whole.

Luis was familiar with the alternation between, on the one hand, times when his thinking was immobilized and inhibited, and, on the other, periods when it raced out of control and left him close to chaos. Most of the time, as far as we could see in the course of his psychoanalytic psychodrama, his thinking was shattered and fragmented. This was quite different from the kind of well-established delusion that patients often try to hide. Luis let us see only a few elements of his delusion, when he told us that he was Mr. D – D as in Demon and in Dante – and that in his land of Darkness there had to be some Lucifer to carry a torch.

In the initial stages of the psychodrama, the excitation and disorganization aroused by the encounter with us led Luis to repeat some words taken out of context and pronounce others that became overloaded and bloated with meaning, to such an extent that they ended up becoming meaningless – language itself was dislocated, as it were. Was that a delusion crumbling away or one that had never succeeded in taking proper shape? It was difficult to decide. For example, he kept on saying that, in the play, he had been "a good performer . . . perforator", letting us catch a glimpse of his obsession with holes that had to be filled up. On one occasion, he suggested that we play out an interview. When we asked him what the object of the interview would be, he replied, satisfied with the tautology of the statement: "An interview . . . for being interviewed". Again, when it was suggested that one of the therapists "do the wall" ("*fasse le mur*") that Luis had just spoken about – in the sense of representing that wall – Luis said that he did not understand because, for him, "faire le mur" ("do the wall") had only one meaning, i.e. run away.[1] Curiously enough, the metaphorical expression that had become a cliché prevailed over the literal meaning that he did not perceive, thus revealing his difficulty in apprehending a word in its connection with a concrete and representable reality.

Words which, as in poetry, belong to another kind of rationality support thinking as regards its potentiality and at the same time hide it; they deploy language but at the same time dismantle and de-structure it. Luis took support from such words; he clung to them when he could no longer feel any sensations – and also when these were too intense and overwhelming, when an over-present reality could not be integrated into the continuity/discontinuity of mental functioning. At that point it became abstract, abstracted and dissolved.

Luis's thinking, which could break up and move towards its own obliteration, could also take on another form, when questions concerning the "why" of his being began to move restlessly around inside him – he would then be in the grip of a compulsion to think that led to abstraction, again in the sense of being abstracted. At that point, there was a hyper-cathexis not only of words but also of thinking – of a certain kind of thinking – in a denial of sexuality, splitting of the ego, cutting himself off. He was at that point on the edge of a precipice which made him stagger, which fascinated him, attracted him and terrified him; to protect himself, he had to construct his own private system, one that would explain his self and the world – a delusion.

As if it were a ritual, at the beginning of one particular session, Luis said how tired he felt, how difficult it was for him to get out of bed to come to his psychodrama sessions, and added that he had no idea inside him of what could be the theme of a play scenario. The play leader suggested that very theme: playing out the lack of ideas or thoughts, what Luis described as a great emptiness. Anonymous "people" would come and admire his emptiness. He chose two therapists: in the play scenario, one represented his physical upset, the pain in his stomach, and asked where the nearest toilet was; the other asked him if he was going to vomit or empty himself. At that point, Luis said that, inside himself, he had a terrifying bottomless chasm. A third therapist came into the play and put his arms round Luis to make a kind of wall to protect him. Luis then said that he felt better, adding that in the pit, the chasm that was inside him, there was a terrible wild animal. In the following session, he explained that the animal in question was not nasty but ugly. The origin of that animal was unknown to him.

We played out various things concerning that animal in several sessions and, depending on the scenario, in different ways. Sometimes we felt that it represented Luis, whose origin was completely unknown, so foreign was he to his being; a monstrous being perhaps, with his difficulty in being accepted and in accepting himself as he was – and also with all of his drive-related violence that we were attempting to tame. He acknowledged that the animal was also the delusion that he had said he wanted to show us but that he had kept hidden until then deep down inside himself in order to fill up a hole, a chasm – all that was unknown about him, all that isolated him and that he translated as ugliness; he was also very proud of it as if it were a very precious possession. A delusion that he wanted to keep, one that simultaneously prevented him from getting close to other people and protected him, made him feel that he existed.

In another scenario, Luis suggested that he could be in a labyrinth with two other people, in confrontation, as he put it, with reality. He refused to leave the labyrinth. He mentioned some windows – the very fact of looking out represented a temptation: being attracted towards the outside; but Luis repeated his refusal to let himself be tempted. That was an extremely ambiguous way of putting things, because outside, after all, there was that wild animal, perhaps a wolf, he said. There was danger on both sides, inside and outside. It was necessary for him to be elsewhere – and he went straight on to say that a delusion is one way of escaping and breaking free of what is felt to be intolerable. He was indeed imprisoned in a paradoxical situation in which the delusional temptation was simply that of a breakaway with no substance to it, no substratum as it were – yet at the same time it was a necessity, because it protected him so that he would not be too affected, so that he would not be in pain.

Psychodrama can give shape to situations that have less to do with something in the patient's past that had proved inaccessible until then than with a paradoxical way of functioning – the patient is simultaneously caught up in an inside/outside that is non-differentiated and dangerous, in an emptiness/fullness that is also overwhelming and in which the nothingness aspect constantly seems to be on the point of emerging. The real danger lies in the withdrawal of the delusional thoughts or in their nothingness – a twofold danger made of emptiness and invasiveness, putting the patient on the edge of a bottomless pit, of an unfathomable and unthinkable emptiness.

There is, nonetheless, a great difference between what is done on the edge of the precipice so as not to fall down inside and the bottom of the pit as it appears in imagination. The poet Paul Valéry, in his introduction to Edgar Allan Poe's "Eureka", has this to say:

> The idea of nothingness is nothingness; or rather, it is already something: it is a pretence of the spirit that gives itself a comedy of silence and of perfect darkness, in which I know full well that I am hidden, ready to create, by a mere slackening of my attention . . . It is an image and it is an act: my name is Nothingness by momentary convention.
>
> (1924, p. 139)

Poets are aware of what is happening inside themselves. There are moments when they feel bereft of any inspiration, but they know that they will come back from that, and there are moments that incite them to be creative. Although this can help us to understand the psychotic mode of functioning, patients themselves are aware only of the dark and hidden face of these moments, the aspect that is the most dangerous. Fragmentation, distortion, hyper-cathexis or abolition of thinking – the delusional temptation is there as an answer to the danger of breaking apart and falling into nothingness.

Luis's strangeness – and, more generally, the relationship that psychotic patients have with words and the surrounding world – did not come, as has been so often but wrongly claimed, from the fact that he functioned in primary-process mode or that his libido had turned back into his ego to such an extent that he found himself in a primitive an-objectal state of narcissism. Psychotic patients have a taste for language and words. They can feel both the exaltation and the horror of thinking. If they often refuse to report their dreams, it is because their dreams are so terrifying and – even more – not sufficiently differentiated from delusional thoughts.

Thoughts that create images

Between the disappointment of nothingness and the vertigo of limitlessness, there are different ways of thinking of oneself and of the world, of thinking about reasons or causes. We can adhere to some mythical, religious or philosophical system as the majority of people do. We can take sexuality as our basis for such issues, as in psychoanalytic theory. We can also construct for ourselves a private system of thought and be delusional or, standing back somewhat from beliefs or convictions, imagine. Imagine – something rather than nothing.

"Imaging" poetical activity is different from delusional thinking because within it there is some degree, no matter how small, of reflexivity. The thought is not "without a thinker", closed in on itself as in delusional thinking with its often-implacable logic. It enables a space to be created in which irrational elements can enter, even if there is as yet no symbolism, which always implies meaning. It is potentially a creation, a sharing.

Imagination, the Muse of poets and artists, takes on the aura of the poetic prestige that is part of delusions and shares to some extent the same exaltation. The fact that images are more predominant than affects means that violence and nameless dread can be kept at a distance. For psychoanalysts, imagining is not the same thing as dreaming. Nor does it amount to fantasizing, in the sense of working through fantasies that reveal the unconscious, linked to repression.

Imagining: not only is it not psychoanalytic in the strict sense of the word, but it carries with it a negative note that verges on belittlement. It is a notion that has a particular place in thinking – that of illusion, of what is artificial and a mere pretence. It is indeed difficult to emphasize the importance and significance of imagination when the word itself immediately awakens the Jungian ghost of active imagination and the collective unconscious, or when it gives us a glimpse of Lacan's Imaginary – of the three categories, Real, Imaginary and Symbolic, the Imaginary one, in Lacan's view, has to yield to the Symbolic. In spite of the silence that has for so long surrounded this topic, is it not time to spring to the defence of the imaging function of thinking and demonstrate how it works?

Winnicott, following Freud, agreed that poets have some special knowledge, and was interested in the idea of imagination. He draws a clear distinction, in *Playing and Reality*, in his discussion of a case of primary dissociation, between "fantasying" and fantasy. Dreaming is not the same as fantasying; in his view, dreaming, a nocturnal activity based on repression, is linked to life, while fantasying, which is closer to day-dreaming, is specific to dissociation and represents an obstacle to life in the real world. That contrast is somewhat different from what Freud suggested in "Creative Writers and Day-Dreaming". In that paper, Freud makes no difference between them; he draws a kind of equivalence between children's play, day-dreaming, fantasy and works of literature, all of them participating in "the three periods of time and the wish which runs through them" (1908 [1907], p. 151).

Winnicott gives the example of a patient who, looking out of the window of her analyst's consulting room, said: "I am up on those pink clouds where I can walk" (1971, p. 27). Then she added, when pressed by Winnicott, who had told her about his theory of such situations:

> When I am walking up on that pink cloud, is that my imagination enriching life or is it this thing that you are calling fantasying which happens when I am doing nothing and which makes me feel that I do not exist?
>
> (ibid., p. 31)

There is probably no better way of describing the very ambiguity of imagination. It is at that point that Winnicott's condemnation of "dreaming activity" (I would rather say "imaging" in the sense of "day-dreaming") appears to contradict what he writes in the chapter entitled "Creativity and its Origins" (1971, p. 65); proof that the boundaries between dreaming, imagining or fantasying and fantasizing always make us think again. With reference to his "dissociated" patient, Winnicott adds (p. 33): "Fantasying possesses her like an evil spirit. From here she went on to her great need to be able to possess herself and to be in possession and to be in control." He adds that her tendency to give herself over to fantasying, which he compares to the idea of formlessness, "*had no poetic value.* The corresponding dream, however, *had poetry in it*" (p. 35 – italics in the original).

In accordance with his idea of regression, Winnicott saw poetry as being linked to primary processes. More than that, indeed, because in his view poetry helps us to make contact, without going as far as primary processes, with the pre-verbal level, with the very source at which poets draw their inspiration:

> We must draw on our experience with psychoanalytic patients who reach back to very early phenomena and yet who can verbalize (when they feel they can do so) without insulting the delicacy of what is preverbal, unverbalized, and unverbalizable except perhaps in poetry.
>
> (1971, p. 112)

Winnicott there places before us an astonishing alternative. It is also an astonishing conception of poetry, which apparently comes into existence, like dreams, only when it is subjected to meaningful interpretations – or else it is a return to the preverbal stage. Coleridge may be able to help us out here. In his view, there are two levels of imagination, which correspond on the one hand to *fancy* and on the other to *imagination* – the latter being on a higher level. "Creative" imagination has the power of harmonizing a multiplicity of elements and drawing them into the primal unity of humankind and the universe.

To return to Luis, I think it appropriate that we should let our thoughts meander; with him, we shall imagine, do some fantasying and fantasize. At the end of one play scene, Luis said that he was surprised at being able to imagine; that happened only on very rare occasions, he added. He mentioned one occasion when, on the bank of a river, he had felt very calm. He was looking at the countryside around him – perhaps the "pink clouds" of Winnicott's patient. He had discovered a space in which he could imagine, in peace and quiet, rather than be delusional with all its noise and fury. He suggested that we play a scenario in which he would be sitting by the sea in order "to be at peace in his peacefulness" and see differences in the blue and green of the sea. A freeze frame . . . focusing on images of "absence as a presence".

In another session, he spoke in a very disjointed way about a film in which, apparently, there was a princess and some unicorns in a forest. The princess was not to approach the unicorns, and certainly not touch them, otherwise she would die. There was also a genie of the forest, a kind of goblin or elf whose word was law. Snow began to fall and the forest started to freeze.

How were we to play out a scenario that appealed so strongly to our interpretative vocation as analysts? In fact, that was just what we did. In the play, a primal scene was obviously present: the princess–unicorn couple wanted to unite and both of them said to the goblin (Luis), who did not allow them to do so, that it was not up to him to decide and anyway that he was too small. A wild animal came on the scene and separated the couple.

I would say that that session was an excellent illustration of the distance with which we function as analysts, of the asymmetry of our position with respect to the need that psychotic patients have for an opening towards the Imaginary in order to have access to it. Psychodrama play is one means of access, not in this case to the symbolic but to that intermediate phase, the imaginary – the imaginary as an intermediary. What Luis gave us to understand – even if we saw in the scenario a primal scene (and the play was pointed in that direction) – was that he was in another space, one that was evoked by the image of the unicorn, a non-existent animal, the origin of which is unknown. Poetical images were emerging, not signifiers – and memory images even less. Therein lay the difference. Luis was showing us how he functioned – and we had to respect that, otherwise he would have been faced with emptiness, disappearance, annihilation. He was also revealing to us how close he could be to poetry.

As time went by, Luis moved from unicorn to sheep – a real, domesticated animal – and proposed a scenario in which he could perhaps identify with a "revolutionary" sheep, one that no longer intended to let itself be pushed around. It wanted to leave the pen because, as Luis pointed out, every sheep ends up by being killed. We could no doubt have accompanied him even further in his imaginary which was just beginning to take shape, and in so doing let him move away from the delusional temptation on the frontier between delusion and imagination.

Recourse to the imaginary enables patients to structure to some extent what is still a confused jumble and to approach their terrifying fears while keeping them at a suitable distance. By letting stories unfold that sometimes have little to do with the patient's real past, psychodrama opens a path to a thought looking for a thinker.

For psychoanalysts, the possible pitfalls with such patients are twofold: either suggesting a symbolizing interpretation that is premature and untimely, or simply accompanying the patient for a long period in the imaginary, as Jung suggested; this ends up being a hindrance to any process of transformation. The analyst must – and this is a difficult part of the work – in a kind of basic asymmetry, keep alive inside him- or herself the path towards an interpretation that links up with infantile sexuality, and at the same time put on hold that interpretative capacity in order to hear what else the patient is expressing, in order to be able to echo what the patient is experiencing. Attunement does not always go without saying – particularly in the case of patients who are in fact very much out of tune.

The Surrealists' idea of "poetic analogy" (Breton, 1948), in which image and myth are seen not as something to be interpreted but as a transition or crossing point, can help us get in touch with the psychotic way of being and open up a path towards one way of understanding it. It enables us to differentiate between Freud's metaphorical or analogical view and one in which the image as such is seen to have an enhanced status. The analytical approach leads to a retrogressive movement, to the earliest forms of thought, while the poetic analogy is a forward-looking movement. The psychoanalytic approach involves the unconscious referent and sees images as a metaphor, in which meanings can be brought together and treated as analogous. For the Surrealists, images involve a transfer of meaning, a substitution, which creates a "truncated" metaphor and, while taking dissociation into account, fills the gap between two terms. With these patients, certain images keep coming back – those that fill up a "hole", plug a crack in a wall, block off a void: something torn or torn off, a skin, weaving, knitting, connecting together. These images correspond very closely to how such patients experience themselves and give shape to what cannot be expressed in words, to what is formless. Others can open up and create a new space.

As we know, words can give rise to fears in psychotic patients and fascinate them. Words may be emptied of all meaning or be frozen in a single meaning – or, on the other hand, be overloaded with meanings to such an extent that they are transformed into signs that are interpretable and persecutory. Access to imaging thinking, which creates images, lies between meaning and non-meaning; these images gradually come to replace chaos and delusional ideas. They represent what Armando Ferrari (2007) has called "metaphorical potential".

In his "Two Versions of the Imaginary", Maurice Blanchot draws a distinction between two kinds of images: the classic ones come on the scene after the object, after the thing, in a presence freed from existence: "In this way the image fills one of its functions, which is to pacify, to humanize the unformed nothingness pushed towards us by the residue of being that cannot be eliminated" (1955b, p. 417). The other kind of image is

> constantly threatening to send us back, no longer to the absent thing, but to absence as presence, to the neutral double of the object, in which belonging to the world has vanished; this duplicity is not such that one can pacify it with an 'either . . . or else . . .'
>
> (pp. 424–425)

Therein lies the ambiguity of images, he writes, which do not involve an "either . . . or else . . .", but a "sometimes, sometimes" (p. 425). It is this that we find in our psychotic patients. From their experience of nothingness, of emptiness, of the stasis of thinking, arises something, even if it is only a silence or a shape, as in a dreamy atmosphere, which coexists with their delusional thoughts.

Michel de M'Uzan's point of view – which has much more to do with the psychoanalytic relationship in its "paradoxical functioning" – is particularly apposite here. After quoting Jean Paulhan – "these spheres without any identity or in which identity is vague or radically different and which actively demand to be filled with meaning" – de M'Uzan continues:

> It must indeed be acknowledged that formlessness is not wholly and uniquely on the side of an absence of being; it is manifested at a point where non-being is a natural position, potentially orientated towards the installation of objects that one day will be able to be named.
>
> (2003 [2005, p. 109])

Not to accept formlessness, what has not yet come to be and has not yet been created, the uncreated – the obverse of something that does have shape, that has come to be and has been created – would imply giving up something that is present in and necessary for every human being. I mean by that a certain kind of imagination, where thoughts ramble along and thinking can be distorted – of course, this could lead to dissociation and relinquishment, but it may also give rise to artistic creation as well as to its delusional counterpart. Such a non-acceptance would mean wanting to fill up at all costs that space which, as long as it does not (it does in extreme cases) provoke horror of a gaping chasm or abyss, is the part of human beings which does not lend itself immediately to symbolizing activity or which does not let itself be caught up in this. Poets and artists have described that experience – Mallarmé, Artaud, Lautréamont . . . They moved out of a narrow channel, pushed back the frontiers of language and reason, aimed for the boundlessness of thinking, of emptiness and also of hatred. What they attempted to bring about was a deconstruction/construction, and they are admired for having done so.

The frontier is indeed a moving one, not easy to define, between emptiness and stereotypes – or, conversely, the inventions that sometimes fill up that emptiness. As is well known, poetry, like delusions, oscillates between ritornellos and original creations. Sometimes delusion and poetry can be looked upon as similar because of their incomprehensible and inaccessible character. In both, there is no possibility of clear thoughts that can be transmitted and translated; there is the same disarticulation between reality and language when it comes to describing and thinking about what lies beyond; there is the same fascination – and fear – that seizes hold of anyone who cares to draw near.

In a posthumous paper, Racamier describes delusional thinking – what he calls "the delusional" – as "a form that belongs to a fourth category of space. Another space, completely different from the internal, external and intermediate reality that make up the other three spaces" (2000). He adds that only a few artists – Bacon and Picabia, for example – have dared to venture into that space.

We should probably indeed think in terms of several spaces side-by-side, spaces that sometimes overlap; the psychoanalyst's task – by no means an easy one – is to go from one to the other. The capturing/letting go (possession/dispossession) of the self that the analyst experiences *a minima* in the classic form of treatment with neurotic patients (the patient lying on the couch) is, in a face-to-face analysis or in psychoanalytic psychodrama, not only amplified but also reinforced. These phenomena are experienced in several spaces which coexist, but which do not necessarily participate in any dualistic thinking. Hence the paradox: one has to be a psychoanalyst to the very depths of one's being to be able not to be one. Psychoanalytic thinking, for each and every one of us, has always to be thought about, again and again.

Notes

Foreword by Bernard Chervet

1 Mary Shelley, with *Frankenstein*; the Surrealists, with Breton; Matisse's paintings; the life-writing of Tristram Shandy (Laurence Sterne's novel); Maurice Blanchot; Georges Bataille, etc.

2 The idealized image of humanism in psychiatry is that of Pinel freeing the insane from their shackles, a gesture that mirrors the emotional attentiveness paid to Victor, the wild boy of Aveyron, by his psychiatrist Jean Itard, a child psychiatrist before the term was ever invented. That tradition was maintained by Henri Ey over and beyond his organo-dynamic approach, as well as by the introduction of outpatient psychiatric clinics, helped of course by the arrival of psychiatric medication, which offered an alternative to being locked up in an asylum. That kind of humanism brings to mind its philosophical counterpart with the Renaissance, Erasmus and Thomas Moore, as expressed in both *In Praise of Folly* and *Utopia*. Humanism consists in acknowledging the dignity of the individual over and beyond pathology, morbidity and insanity. In the ethics of humanism, nosography, with its tables, descriptions and structures, tends to fade into the background; what comes more to the fore are ideas such as potentiality, position, solution, temptation. The essence of this approach is to lend support to the existence of individuals who are subjected to their destiny, to the tragedy of what tends to make them lose all notion of themselves.

3 Herbert Rosenfeld, Jean-Luc Donnet and André Green, Piera Aulagnier, Michel de M'Uzan, Winnicott, Bion, etc.

4 Underlying the psychotic solution, there are issues to do with the *missing link*, the impossibility of responding to all of these drive-related demands simply through the act of representing, and the importance of the concept of psychical processing and the means to accomplish it.

Rifts in the ego

1 An allusion to the title of one of André Breton's writings, "Limits not frontiers of surrealism" (Breton, 1937).

1 The question of origins

1 A reference to the title of a recent issue of *Penser/Rêver – La Fabrique de l'origine* [*Thinking/Dreaming – Fabricating origins*], no. 10, 2001.

2 "We can divide the life of each instinct into a series of separate successive waves, each of which is homogeneous during whatever period of time it may last, and whose relation to one another is comparable to that of successive eruptions of lava. We can then perhaps picture the first, original eruption of the instinct as proceeding in an unchanged form and undergoing no development at all. The next wave would be modified from the outset – being turned, for instance, from active to passive – and would then, with this new characteristic, be added to the earlier wave, and so on" (Freud, 1915c, p. 131).

3 Literally, a brothel; it is also used colloquially to mean a shambles. (Translator's note)

2 When going back is impossible

1 Freud did, however, in his study of aphasia (1891), say the opposite: whatever lies at a lower stage – and is therefore earlier – is more organized.

2 It is important here to draw the reader's attention to the twofold valency of the word "agony" in English – it can mean both a paroxysm of grief/anguish and an intensity or paroxysm of pleasure.

3 "Actual-ness", broken time, time in confusion

1 The literal meaning of the colloquial phrase employed by Mr. A is: "having a little bicycle in [his] head". (Translator's note)

4 Correspondence

1 The French term for "pending" or "waiting to be dealt with" is "*en souffrance*", with its evocation of "suffering" (Translator's note).

2 Cf. *Lettres à une religieuse portugaise* [*Letters to a Portuguese Nun*] in 1669 and, in the same year, *Lettres à Barbet* [*Letters to Barbet*] by Boursault.

5 The materiality of writing

1 It originates in Middle English, coming via Old French from medieval Latin: *trepalium* "instrument of torture", which derives from the Latin *tres* "three" + *palus* "stake".

8 The delusional temptation and imaging thinking

1 In colloquial French, "*faire le mur*" means "to go over the wall", in other words to run away, to escape. (Translator's note)

References

Aragon, L. (1924). *Une vague de rêves*. Paris: Seghers, 1990; reprinted 2006 [*A Wave of Dreams*, trans. A. Cornford]. Sausalito, CA: Duration Press.

Artaud, A. (1974). "Ci-Gît", in *Oeuvres Complètes*, Vol. XII. Paris: Gallimard.

Aulagnier, P. (1975). *La violence de l'interprétation. Du pictogramme à l'énoncé*. Paris: Presses Universitaires de France [*The Violence of Interpretation: From Pictogram to Statement*, trans. A. Sheridan]. London: Routledge, 2001.

Aulagnier, P. (1984). *L'apprenti historien et le maître sorcier* [*The Apprentice Historian and the Master Sorcerer*]. Paris: Presses Universitaires de France.

Barthes, R. (1980). "La chambre claire; note sur la photographie", in *Cahiers du Cinéma*, Paris: Gallimard [*Camera Lucida; Reflections on Photography*]. London: Vintage, 1993.

Beckett, S. (1958). *Malone Dies. Three Novels: Molloy, Malone Dies, The Unnamable*. New York: Grove Press.

Bion, W. R. (1967). *Second Thoughts: Selected Papers on Psycho-Analysis*. London: Heinemann, reprinted London: Karnac, 1984.

Blanchot, M. (1955a). *L'espace littéraire*. Paris: Gallimard [*The Space of Literature*, trans. A. Smock]. Lincoln, NE: University of Nebraska Press, 1982.

Blanchot, M. (1955b). "Two versions of the imaginary", appendix to *The Space of Literature*, trans. A. Smock. Lincoln, NE: University of Nebraska Press, 1982.

Blanchot, M. (1982). "Le trouble de penser" ["Disorder of thinking"]. *Nouvelle Revue de Psychanalyse*, no. 25, Spring.

Breton, A. (1937). "Limites non frontières du surréalisme". Paris: NRF ["Limits not frontiers of surrealism", in *Surrealism*, ed. H. Read]. London: Faber & Faber, 1936.

Breton, A. (1948). "Signe ascendant". Paris: Gallimard, 1968 ["Ascendant sign", in *Free Rein*, trans. M. Parmentier and J. d'Amboise]. Lincoln, NE: University of Nebraska Press, 1995.

Breton, A. (1963). *Manifeste du surréalisme.* Paris: Gallimard [*Manifestoes of Surrealism*, trans. R. Seaver and H. R. Lane]. Ann Arbor, MI: University of Michigan Press, 1969.

Breton, A. (1970). *Le point du jour.* Paris: Gallimard [*Break of Day*, trans. M. Polizzotti and M. A. Caws]. Lincoln, NE: University of Nebraska Press, 1999.

Burke, E. (1909–1914). *A Philosophical Inquiry into the Origin of Our Ideas of the Sublime and Beautiful.* New York: Collier.

Celan, P. (2001). "No-One's-Rose", in *Selected Poems and Prose of Paul Celan*, trans. J. Felstiner. New York: Norton.

Cheng, F. (1996). *L'écriture poétique chinoise.* Paris: Le Seuil. [*Chinese Poetic Writing, with an Anthology of T'ang Poetry*, trans. D. A. Riggs & J. P. Seaton]. Bloomington, IN: Indiana University Press, 1982.

Chervet, B. (2008). "La sexualité infantile en souffrance et les topiques éclatées". *Revue française de psychanalyse*, LXXII, no. 3, pp. 707–729.

Chervet, B. (2009). "L'après-coup. La tentative d'inscrire ce qui tend à disparaître". *Revue française de psychanalyse*, LXXIII, no. 5 (special Congress issue), pp. 1361–1441.

Deleuze, G. (1993). "La littérature et la vie", in *Critique et clinique.* Paris: Éditions de Minuit ["Literature and life", trans. D. W. Smith & M. A. Greco], in *Critical Inquiry*, 23, no. 2, Winter 1997.

Donnet, J. L. and Green, A. (1973). *L'enfant de ça* [*The Child of That/of the Id*]. Paris: Minuit.

Dubois, P. (1990). *L'acte photographique* [*The Photographic Act*]. Paris: Nathan.

Eluard, P. (1926). *Capitale de la douleur.* Paris: Gallimard, 1966 [*Capital of Pain*, trans. R. M. Weisman]. New York: Grossman, 1973.

Enriquez, M. (1978). "L'indicible et l'écriture" ["Writing and what cannot be expressed in words"]. *Topique.* Also in Enriquez, M. (2001). *La souffrance et la haine, paranoia, masochisme, apathie* [*Suffering and Hate, Paranoia, Masochism, Apathy*]. Paris: Dunod.

Enriquez, M. (2001). *La souffrance et la haine, paranoia, masochisme, apathie* [*Suffering and Hate, Paranoia, Masochism, Apathy*]. Paris: Dunod.

Ertel, R. (1993). *Dans la langue de personne. Poésie yiddish de l'anéantissement* [*In the Language of No-One: Yiddish Poetry of Annihilation*]. Paris: Le Seuil.

Fabre, D. (1993). *Écritures ordinaires* [*Ordinary Writings*]. Paris: POL.

Federn, P. (1952). *Ego Psychology and the Psychoses* (ed. E Weiss). New York: Basic Books [London: Imago, 1953].

Ferenczi, S. (1916). Letter from Sándor Ferenczi to Sigmund Freud, April 27, 1916. In *The Correspondence of Sigmund Freud and Sandor Ferenczi Vol. 2, 1914–1919* (ed. E. Falzeder and E. Brabant). Cambridge, MA: Harvard University Press, 1996.

Ferenczi, S. (1938). *Thalassa: A Theory of Genitality* (trans. H. A. Bunker). London: Karnac, 1989.

Ferenczi, S. (1949). "Confusion of tongues between adult and child". *International Journal of Psycho-Analysis*, 30: 225–230.
Ferenczi, S. (1955). *Final Contributions to the Problems and Methods of Psychoanalysis. The Selected Papers of Sandor Ferenczi, M.D. Vol. III* (ed. M. Balint). New York: Basic Books [London: Karnac, 1994].
Ferrari, A. (2007). *La Metafora nel linguaggio della relazione analitica* [*Metaphor in the Language of the Analytical Relationship*]. Milan: Mimesis edizioni.
Fonyi, A. (1994). *Lire, écrire, analyser* [*Read, Write, Analyse*]. Paris: L'Harmattan.
Freud, S. (1891). *ZurAuffassung der Aphasien* [*On Aphasia: A Critical Study*]. New York: International Universities Press, 1953.
Freud, S. (1895 [1893–1895]). *Studies on Hysteria. Standard Edition*, 2.
Freud, S. (1899). Letter from Freud to Fliess, August 6, 1899. In *The Complete Letters of Sigmund Freud to Wilhelm Fliess, 1887–1904* (ed. J. M. Masson). Cambridge, MA: The Belknap Press of Harvard University Press, 1985.
Freud, S. (1900). *The Interpretation of Dreams. Standard Edition*, 4 and 5.
Freud, S. (1905a). *Jokes and Their Relation to the Unconscious. Standard Edition*, 8.
Freud, S. (1905b). *Three Essays on the Theory of Sexuality. Standard Edition*, 7: 125.
Freud, S. (1905c [1901]). "Fragment of an Analysis of a Case of Hysteria". *Standard Edition*, 7: 3.
Freud, S. (1908 [1907]). "Creative Writers and Day-Dreaming". *Standard Edition*, 9: 143.
Freud, S. (1910). *Leonardo da Vinci and a Memory of his Childhood. Standard Edition*, 11: 59.
Freud, S. (1911). "The Case of Schreber, Papers on Technique and Other Works, ii–vii". In *The Standard Edition of the Complete Psychological Works of Sigmund Freud, Volume XII (1911–1913).* The Hogarth Press and the Institute of Psychoanalysis: London.
Freud, S. (1912). "The Dynamics of Transference". *Standard Edition*, 12: 99.
Freud, S. (1912–1913). *Totem and Taboo. Standard Edition*, 13: ix.
Freud, S. (1913). "The Theme of the Three Caskets". *Standard Edition*, 12: 291.
Freud, S. (1914a). "The Moses of Michelangelo". *Standard Edition*, 13: 211.
Freud, S. (1914b). "Remembering, Repeating and Working-Through (Further Recommendations on the Technique of Psycho-Analysis, II)". *Standard Edition*, 12: 147.
Freud, S. (1915a [1914]). "Observations on Transference-Love (Further Recommendations on the Technique of Psycho-Analysis, III)". *Standard Edition*, 12: 159.
Freud, S. (1915b). "The Unconscious". *Standard Edition*, 14: 161.
Freud, S. (1915c). "Instincts and Their Vicissitudes". *Standard Edition*, 14: 111.

Freud, S. (1915d). "A Case of Paranoia Running Counter to the Psycho-Analytic Theory of the Disease". *Standard Edition*, 14: 263.
Freud, S. (1916 [1915]). "On Transience". *Standard Edition*, 14: 305.
Freud, S. (1916–1917 [1915–1917]). *Introductory Lectures on Psycho-Analysis. Standard Edition*, 15 and 16.
Freud, S. (1917a [1915]). "A Metapsychological Supplement to the Theory of Dreams". *Standard Edition*, 14: 219.
Freud, S. (1917b [1915]). "Mourning and Melancholia". *Standard Edition*, 14: 239.
Freud, S. (1918 [1914]). "From the History of an Infantile Neurosis". *Standard Edition*, 17: 3.
Freud, S. (1919 [2010]). "The Uncanny". *Standard Edition*, 17: 219.
Freud, S. (1920). *Beyond the Pleasure Principle. Standard Edition*, 18: 1.
Freud, S. (1923 [1922]). "Two Encyclopaedia Articles. (A) Psycho-Analysis; (B) The Libido Theory". *Standard Edition*, 18: 235 and 255.
Freud, S. (1924a). "The Loss of Reality in Neurosis and Psychosis". *Standard Edition*, 19: 183.
Freud, S. (1924b [1923]). "Neurosis and Psychosis". *Standard Edition*, 19: 149.
Freud, S. (1925a [1924]). "A Note upon the 'Mystic Writing-Pad' ". *Standard Edition*, 19: 227.
Freud, S. (1925b [1924]). *An Autobiographical Study. Standard Edition*, 20: 3.
Freud, S. (1925c). "Negation". *Standard Edition*, 19: 235.
Freud, S. (1926a [1925]). *Inhibitions, Symptoms and Anxiety. Standard Edition*, 20: 77.
Freud, S. (1926b). *The Question of Lay Analysis. Standard Edition*, 20: 179.
Freud, S. (1933a [1932]). *New Introductory Lectures on Psycho-Analysis. Standard Edition*, 22: 3.
Freud, S. (1933b [1932]). "Why War?" [with A. Einstein]. *Standard Edition*, 22: 197.
Freud, S. (1934). Letter from Freud to Arnold Zweig, May 12, 1934. In *The Letters of Sigmund Freud and Arnold Zweig* (ed. E. L. Freud). London: The Hogarth Press and the Institute of Psycho-Analysis, 1970.
Freud, S. (1937). "Constructions in Analysis". *Standard Edition*, 23: 257.
Freud, S. (1939 [1937–1939]). *Moses and Monotheism. Three Essays. Standard Edition*, 23: 3.
Freud, S. (1940a [1938]). *An Outline of Psycho-Analysis. Standard Edition*, 23:141
Freud, S. (1940b [1938]). "Splitting of the Ego in the Process of Defence". *Standard Edition*, 23: 273.
Freud, S. (1950 [1895]). "Project for a Scientific Psychology". *Standard Edition*, 1: 283.
Green, A. (2003). *Le travail psychanalytique* [*The Work of Psychoanalysis*]. Paris: Presses Universitaires de France.

Kestemberg, E. (1972). Paper presented at the Paris International Symposium on *The Long-term Treatment of Psychotic States* (ed. C. Chiland and P. Bequart). Paris: Privat, 1974.

Kestemberg, E. (1978). "La relation fétichique à l'objet" ["The fetishistic object relationship"]. In *La psychose froide* [*Cold Psychosis*] (pp. 77–101). Paris: Presses Universitaires de France, 2001. Also in *Reading French Psychoanalysis* (ed. D. Birksted-Breen, S. Flanders and A. Gibeault). London: Routledge, 2010.

Kestemberg, E. (1981). "'L'appareil' psychique et les organisations psychiques diverses" ["The 'psychic apparatus' in various mental structures"]. In *La psychose froide* [*Cold Psychosis*] (pp. 179–199). Paris: Presses Universitaires de France, 2001.

Kestemberg, E. (2001). *La psychose froide* [*Cold Psychosis*]. Paris: Presse Universitaires de France.

Kestemberg, E., Kestemberg, J. and Decobert, S. (1972). *La faim et le corps* [*Hunger and the Body*]. Paris: Presses Universitaires de France.

Laplanche, J. and Pontalis, J. B. (1968). "Fantasy and the origins of sexuality". *International Journal of Psycho-Analysis*, 49: 1–18.

Laplanche, J. and Pontalis, J. B. (1973). *The Language of Psychoanalysis*. London: The Hogarth Press and the Institute of Psycho-Analysis.

Leclaire, S. (1975). *On tue un enfant*. Paris: Points-Editions de Seuil [*A Child is Being Killed: On Primary Narcissism and the Death Drive*]. Stanford, CA: Stanford University Press, 1998.

Little, M. (1986). *Transference Neurosis and Transference Psychosis: Towards Basic Unity*. London: Free Association Books.

Mallarmé, S. (1864). "Brise marine" ["Sea beeze"], in *Le Parnasse contemporain*. Paris: Alphonse Lemerre.

Merleau-Ponty, M. (1961). "L'oeil et l'esprit". *Art de Frana I*, no. I. Reprinted Paris: Gallimard, 1964 ["The eye and the mind", in Merleau-Ponty, M. (1964). *The Primacy of Perception* (ed. J. M. Edie, trans. C. Dallery)]. Evanston, IL: Northwestern University Press. Revised by M. Smith in *The Merleau-Ponty Aesthetics Reader* (ed. G. A. Johnson). Evanston, IL: Northwestern University Press, 1993.

M'Uzan, M. de (2003). "De l'informe avant toute chose . . ." ["Formless before anything else . . ."], in *Aux confins de l'identité* [*At the Frontiers of Identity*]. Paris: Gallimard, 2005.

M'Uzan, M. de (2005). *Aux confins de l'identité* [*At the Frontiers of Identity*]. Paris: Gallimard.

Nerval, G. (1853). "El Desdichado" ["The disinherited"], in *Les Chimères*. Paris: Garnier-Flammarion, 1984 [*The Chimeras*. London: Anvil, 1984].

Nicholson, G. (1999). *Plato's Phaedrus: The Philosophy of Love*. West Lafayette, IN: Purdue University Press.

Perron, R. (2003). *La passion des origines. Être et ne pas être* [*The Passion of Origins: To Be and Not To Be*]. Paris: Delachaux & Niestlé.

Poe, E. A. (1839). *The Fall of the House of Usher*, revised edition. Harmondsworth: Penguin Classics, 2003.

Proust, M. (1927). *Le temps retrouvé*. Paris: Gallimard, 2000 [*The Past Recaptured*, trans. A. Mayor]. New York: Random House, 1970.

Racamier, P.-C. (1989). *Anteoedipe et ses destins* (*Antoedipus and its Vicissitudes*). Paris: Apsygee éditions.

Racamier, P.-C. (1992). *Le génie des origines. Psychanalyse et psychoses* [*The Genius of Origins: Psychoanalysis and the Psychoses*]. Paris: Payot.

Racamier, P.-C. (2000). "Un espace pour délirer" ["A space for being delusional"], in *Revue française de Psychanalyse*. Paris: PUF.

Rosenfeld, H. (1952). "Transference-phenomena and transference-analysis in an acute catatonic schizophrenic patient". *International Journal of Psycho-Analysis*, 33: 457–464. Also in H. Rosenfeld, *Psychotic States: A Psycho-Analytical Approach*. London: Hogarth Press/New York: International Universities Press, 1965.

Shelley, M. (1818). *Frankenstein*. Oxford: Oxford University Press, 2008.

Shelley, M. (1826). *The Last Man* (ed. M. D. Paley). Oxford: Oxford Paperbacks, 1998.

Sterne, L. (1759). *The Life and Opinions of Tristram Shandy, Gentleman*. Harmondsworth: Penguin Classics, 2003.

Valéry, P. (1924). "Au sujet d'Eurêka". *Variété I*. Paris: Gallimard ["On Poe's 'Eureka' ", in *The Recognition of Edgar Allan Poe: Selected Criticism Since 1829*, ed. E. Carlson]. Ann Arbor, MI: University of Michigan Press, 1969.

Wagner, G. (1974). *Selected Poems of Charles Baudelaire*. New York: Grove Press.

Winnicott, D. W. (1947). "Hate in the vountertransference", in *Through Paediatrics to Psychoanalysis: Collected Papers*. London: Karnac, 1984.

Winnicott, D. W. (1954). "Withdrawal and regression", in *Through Paediatrics to Psychoanalysis: Collected Papers*. London: Karnac, 1984.

Winnicott, D. W. (1971). *Playing and Reality*. London: Tavistock Publications. Reprinted London: Routledge, 1982.

Winnicott, D. (1974). "Fear of breakdown". *International Review of Psycho-Analysis*, 1: 103–107.

Index